Letters To Ben

by Chris Lockwood

Copyright © 2014 by Chris Lockwood
All rights reserved.
Published in the United States of America
by Chris Lockwood
LettersToBen.com

ISBN 13: 978-0-692-32892-7

Printed in the United States of America

Book Design by Chris Lockwood
Cover Design by Chris Lockwood

First Edition

To Ben and Matt, you never cease to amaze, inspire and motivate me to be a better man.

Thank you.

Contents

Preface: The Beginning	9
Part 1: Essentials For Living A Good Life	21
Part 2: Being Human	51
Part 3: Achievement	84
Part 4: Passion	123
Part 5: Happiness	137
Part 6: Personal Growth	163
Part 7: The Things They Don't Teach You In School	199
Afterword	217
Quote Garden	220

Letters To Ben

Preface

Letters to Ben Introduction

This book was written with the intention of providing my son's some in depth wisdom that most people fail to pass on to their children for one reason or another. As the book began to take shape, I realized that most of what I'm writing about and had intended only for my sons really was valuable to so many people. And that's the reason I chose to print and distribute my book to a larger audience.

Throughout the book you'll find a ton of references to Ben, my oldest son, who I had initially began writing this book for. While it's written to him, the advice is still much the same for you no matter where you are in your life. Take it, shape it for yourself and make it your own.

Enjoy!

....

Ben, I'm going to impart a lot of wisdom on you as you grow up, but this is what I know up to this point and it's in print, so it will be a little more difficult for you to avoid. If you ever need advice and I reference a page number, feel free to roll your eyes, but then dutifully study that section.

What this book is.

When I started writing this book, I had intended for it to be a short and simple way for me to pass on as much of my wisdom as I possibly could for you. It's grown a bit from the initial concept, but it's still going to be relatively short and sweet.

Very little of what's in here is in a long format, mostly because the lessons that are being taught can be summed up nicely in short format. You'll get the long form version directly from me as you grow up, make mistakes and need the advice first hand.

I want this to be a book you can go to for advice when you're most in need and I'm not easily accessible for some reason. It's not a manual for life, but rather the foot notes. Growing up is hard enough, if you can take even a small fraction of what's in this book and apply it to your life, it should save you a lot of pain and frustration.

Take what you need, dismiss what you don't, but when you take my advice, cherish it and use it as though you were the one who gained it through first-hand experience.

What this book is not.

This book is meant to be a guide, a way for you to shortcut yourself to success faster than anyone else can. But that doesn't mean it's a manual that you MUST follow. Things will be different by the time you get old enough to understand everything in here, most of this will still apply, but some may not. No matter how much I wish I could set you up for a lifetime of success, I can't. Most of it will be weight you will have to bare, and you'll have to trudge your own path through the blizzard that is life.

So don't take this book and expect everything in it to mean you'll reach immediate success, because you won't. I believe strongly in learning from others to get yourself to the top as fast as you can, but I also know that behind those shortcuts, there is still a ton of hard work to be completed.

For those of you that may be reading this book but aren't my son, these rules still apply. There will be a lot of value in what you read in this book, but I can't guarantee you anything, only you can guarantee yourself that through hard work and perseverance. Everything I've included in here was based on my experiences, education and personal motivation. Those are all things that I can't easily give to you, but you can learn and create your own experiences if you're motivated.

Who Am I?

I am a die-hard nature lover. It's really the core of who I am and what I love about being here on this planet. And yet, I have failed to set up my life to take hold of this passion. Which is what part of this transformation I'm going through is all about.

It's easy to get sidetracked by living the life you think you want. When I was 18, the job as a 911 dispatcher was an amazing opportunity. I doubled my hourly wage and work hours in an instant from the golf course I was working at, had the power to save people's lives and property and I loved the job.

When I first started working there, I was in my glory. Now that I look at new hires, I can see that I was probably much the same way. In total awe that they actually have to pay people to do that job. It seemed like the perfect place to be able to work, you're the life blood of every single organization that you cover. Without dispatchers there to answer the calls, no one would be able to respond. And on a rare occasion, we're actually able to give instructions that save someone's life.

It's not something I talk about much. It's just a given, and the people I have surrounded myself with up to this point in my life have all been in the same line of work, police officers, firefighters, emt's and paramedics. It's still exciting to be able to save someone's life, prevent a building from burning to the ground or getting an accident victim help, but it doesn't motivate me in the same way it used to.

Don't get me wrong, I'm very proud of the work I do. It's not a job that everyone can handle, but it's just become so "routine" to do these things that there's little fanfare left in it. I've reached my 10,000 hours and what Malcom Gladwell would then refer to as 'Expert Status'. And perhaps that's why I so desperately seek to shake things up. I want to feel alive again, and be inspired. And thankfully I'm getting closer and closer to reaching that goal.

But that's only come by me realizing that public safety is not my entire life, and most likely not what I was put here on earth to accomplish. I'm sure I will forever be involved in it in some respect, I love being a volunteer firefighter, but it's not the BIG picture that I need to be striving for, at least not right now.

I'm still figuring out the who I am part. I think most of us fill forever be doing that as we grow into newer and ever better people throughout our lives. What I do know for sure is that I'm a father, a partner to Susannah, an inspiration to many, a cornerstone for others when times are tough and a protector of the wild. Those are the big things that make up my life.

Why I Chose To Write This Book

Randy Pausch. He gave a 'Last Lecture' speech that ran through my heart. He was so passionate and motivated about being able to be up there to get everything out in the open for his children. He was dying of pancreatic cancer, and realized that he wanted to leave a lasting memory to his children, who were quite young at the time.

The thought of ever having to do that didn't sit easy with me. Really, how do you sit down, write a speech to sum up your entire life, be entertaining and still instill lessons in it for your children that nobody else caught? It was incredible.

And that got me to thinking. So many people wait until they're knocking on deaths door with a sledge hammer to begin compiling their thoughts and looking back at what really matters in this life. I didn't want to become that same person, so I decided I needed to get started on this project long before those days ever came for me.

Do I really feel like I have all the wisdom I'll ever need to express to you yet? Of course not. I'd be a fool to think that. But what I can tell you is that in the short time I have been around, I've learned plenty to provide you with a great starting point.

This was never meant to be the road map for your entire life. It's not designed to be a master plan so when you have a problem like a broken heart you can look up how to cure it. Sorry. But the best way you will learn that is through experiencing it first-hand. The best I am hoping for with this is to provide you guidance, wisdom and the opportunity to grow yourself through my personal experiences.

And hopefully that will be enough. If not…. Well, let me know and I'll have to start sketching ideas for another book that can fix all of life's problems for you. Or better yet, try taking some of the advice here and living it out in your life and let me know how it goes.

So that's the heart of why I'm writing this book. To inspire, motivate and encourage you to live the greatest life you possibly can because I know it's inside you to do that, I'm just hoping my words help you a little bit along the way.

....
"Once we believe in ourselves, we can risk curiosity, wonder, spontaneous delight, or any experience that reveals the human spirit." - E.E. Cummings
....

Letter#1 April 1 2013

April 1, 2013

It seems somewhat odd to be starting such a serious project on April fool's day, but there's no better time to start telling you all about the world than a day that I decide to do something. You see Ben, I've been meaning to start writing for you, for quite a while, but for the longest time I always had trouble starting and staying on track with projects.

I'm what you would call a habitual procrastinator. For some reason I've always felt that I would do better work and enjoy myself a hundred times more by putting off work rather than getting it done. Well, that mentality hasn't gotten me nearly as far in life as I would have liked by this point. But that's all part of the journey of what life is about right? We have to learn to overcome and work beyond our self-imposed limitations, that's the only way we can truly grow as people and as a society.

So I'm not entirely sure where these letters to you will take us, I'm sure there will be stories about our experiences, some triumphs and failures, but it will be exciting. I think the most exciting part of this is that I can begin to impart the wisdom I've learned down to you, and that won't be an easy process.

Not because I know everything there is to know. Far from that. But mostly because I will be trying to figure out how to convey these thoughts and ideas, and how to present them in a way that my message is clear but you'll be able to understand and use them. See, the whole idea is that if I can pass down my wisdom, my experiences and my knowledge bit by bit to you, it should take years off of the learning curve you'll face.

Now I don't want that to be a path for you to take the easy way out and just read some of Dad's wisdom and you'll be fine. That's not at all what this is meant for. It's going to help you propel yourself further than anyone else your age when you take these messages and implement them. Take MASSIVE ACTION.

Don't just learn and never use those things. I've done that for far too long. I thought it was vital to keep studying nonstop, always learning, always finding something new or a new way to do it. But I never implemented it, so all of that learning was essentially useless. Unless you apply the knowledge you gain, you've wasted your time, and your time is a terrible thing to waste. You simply can't get it back, no matter how hard you try.

So with that, I want to start these "Letters to Ben" as I'm calling them with telling you that I need you to always take action. If you want to learn a new skill or sport, go do it, if you want to lose weight or make more money, find a way and then do it, if you want to travel, go do it. But most of all, be sure to do the things that you want to do.

This life is about more than just making a ton of money or working endless hours. Let me tell you one thing, I stopped working overtime when you came around, so I could spend more time with my family, and it was the best decision I could have made. I vowed to minimize the number of major life moments I might miss out on because of work, and so far that has been an amazing life decision.

Another side note on this, I implore you to make your life about how you can provide value to others. I'm not saying you need to travel 3,000 miles away and become a Buddhist monk (unless you want to), but find ways you can consistently provide greater value to others and you will live a much more fulfilled life.

I've spent the better part of 12 years as a volunteer fire fighter, giving it up temporarily when you came along as I adjusted to my new life. But those 12 years were some of the absolute best I had, I sacrificed a lot in that time to help other people, but it was always worth it. I'll talk a lot more about that experience as we go on in these letters, but for now, let's end with those thoughts.

From this point forward, I chose to remove the Letter numbers to simplify the formatting for the book.

Provide consistent value to others lives, take massive action, don't ever waste your time and be sure to live your life for you.

Part One: Essentials For Living A Good Life

Essentials For Living A Good Life

I had originally termed this part of the book 'The Core Of Life' and I struggled over and over how to write the intro for that section. And then I realized that it's not really about the core of life because we all operate from a different and very unique core. The things that motivate, inspire and move me may not be the very same for you.

Yes, for the most part we all share some core things like being a good person, living responsibly, being nice to others, etc, but this section digs deeper than just those things. The elements that make up part 1 of this book are really things that I believe deep down make a difference in just living your life and truly, deeply living a good life.

The reality is that whenever our time is up, whether it's incredibly early on or we're blessed with a very long life, we all want to know we lived a good life right? There are a lot of ways to define what a good life means, and I'll leave that up to you to really decide what you want your life to look like, but I feel deep down at least some of these things should be core elements to it.

I didn't truly realize how important and vital it was to my success to create a lifestyle that I intentionally designed until I was 28. To many, that may seem young, to me that seems late, but that doesn't really matter. All that truly matters is that when you reach that point in your life where you know there has to be more out there than what you're currently experiencing is that you set out to achieve it.

Here's to many amazing years ahead, and may we fill them with fun, laughter, learning and intentional lifestyle design.

Don't Wait Until You're Dying

Don't wait until you're dying to do the things you've always wanted to do.

I'm writing this book for a big reason. It's entirely for you and your brother to read and understand who I am, how I got to where I am today and the best lessons I've learned along the way. I read a book and saw a speech (Last Lecture) by a man name Randy Pausch. He was a professor at Carnegie Mellon University, but long story short, he ended up dying of pancreatic cancer.

He wrote a similar short book for his children, the problem I saw was that he wrote it when he was dying. I didn't want to have to be in that situation to do that for you. I wanted you to have an inspired book that you could use as a tool for the rest of your life. Too many people wait until they're dying to try and squeeze in experiences they always wished they had. I want to encourage you not to do that. Get out there and do the things you want to do. Create a bucket list and check things off of it consistently. Always keep adding to your list so you never run out of experiences you want to live through.

It's a simple idea really, but if you consistently keep adding things to your list and checking off others, it's almost impossible to live a life that wasn't full of amazing experiences. Have both big and small ideas on your list so you can stay focused on it. If it's all full of big ideas, like Walk the Great Wall of China, it's easy to forget about it once it's created because you can create so many barriers to achieving those things. You want to want to find yourself going back to it on a regular basis.

The Power Of Creativity

Long ago, when I was a kid, the world was full of wonder, imagination and just about anything I could dream up. It was the most fantastic feeling in the world, even if I was playing with my toy cars as you do now, they could have been driving up massive mountains, across deserts or under the ocean. It didn't really matter, because it was my world, and things could do whatever I wanted them to do.

That's one of the best parts about being young, you can imagine anything and it seems like reality. Somewhere along the line, as we get older and get "institutionalized" by school, a rigorous lifestyle, non-stop errands, we seem to lose touch with this part of our life. And that's a damn shame.

For most adults, they are stuck on such a routine of get up, get the kids out the door to school, shuffle off to work, be a drone for the day doing mundane tasks, come home, make dinner, put kids to bed, put yourself to bed. This goes on day in and day out, week after week until they are suddenly retired and realize they forgot to live their life.

So the real reason I'm writing about creativity is that it can take this mundane life, put it upside down and shift your life really something exciting. Whether you want to be a painter, a musician or even if you enjoy working with numbers, you can create the life you want.

Don't be afraid to challenge the norms, think outside of the box and blaze your own path through life. Your mind holds an almost unlimited power, it really is up to you to use it to create the world you want to live in.

For years I had always said I would never want an office job. Around the age of 26 I realized I had the absolute worst type of office job I could ever be in. I was stuck in a small room with one other person, and I couldn't even get up to leave for more than a few minutes at a time because of the potential of what might happen.

It became very evident after some searching and looking at what was available for jobs in Connecticut that I needed to create my own life. As I write this, I'm still not 100% confident in what I'm going to do, but I do know I've put my creativity to work lately, and it's been the best thing I could have ever done.

I'm open to new ideas, creating things that I want to experience and designing my life to fit my goals, not someone else's. See Ben, that's the power of creativity, it gives you freedom, freedom from what others may want you to do, freedom from what the world thinks you should be doing and freedom to be what you want to be.

I read not too long ago, how important it is to create your own destiny, otherwise someone else will do it for you, and it will fit their goals, not yours. How true that is.

So open up your mind, put your brain into high gear and think.

Some of the best tips I have when you're trying to be creative are below. This is just what I've found works for me, and I hope someday some of it will work for you, but if not, don't worry, you will find what opens your mind and drives your soul to be creative.

- Get outside - My absolute best thoughts and most creative ideas have always come while walking, hiking or sitting in a peaceful spot outside, never while watching tv, sitting online or otherwise being distracted.

- Write everything down - No matter how 'dumb' you may think it is at the moment, write your ideas down. Someday you will get forgetful and every last idea will serve to rekindle your memory or even better help you think of new and greater things.
- Tap into others ideas - Be a student of other people. Be open and truly listen to what people have to say, they will create new thoughts, ideas and even inspire you.
- Be humble - Some of the most creative people in the world have been the most humble as well. To live a truly fulfilled life, you don't need to be showing off everything you have.
- Music - Find music that inspires and motivates you, listen to it and let your mind wander a bit, it will take you to some interesting places.

Why I Believe In You

This section is going to be rather short and succinct, because I think it's quite easy to explain. I've been on an amazing journey over the last year or so that has opened my eyes to the real value of life and how much more it has to offer than 99% of the world will ever truly realize. My hope is that these letters will get you to that 1% that really understands the power of being alive at this point in time, but ultimately you'll have to get there on your own. The best I can do is guide you.

I believe in you. I know you can achieve anything you set your mind to. And I promise I will always help you get where you want to be in some way. You see Ben, I learned a secret not long ago from a very bright man. I wish I could have met him in person, alas his time came and went well before mine, but his passion and purpose remained locked in some of the world's best books.

I can't even begin to recall the series of events that lead to the discovery of this man and his life's work, but it has been one of the best discoveries a man could make. I fully believe that your mind must be open and willing to receive his messages before you can fully comprehend and understand the power of everything he will tell you.

His name is Napoleon Hill, and he is known the world over as one of the greatest thinkers. He spent nearly 35 years of his life researching, interviewing and piecing together ideas from some of the most successful people in the world at the time. People that have achieved fortunes so vast, we could only dream about seeing those sums in our bank accounts.

You may be thinking to yourself, that's great, but how is any of this going to help me, and what does this have to do with you believing in me? Let me explain.

One of Napoleon's most well-known sayings is "Whatever the mind can conceive and believe, it can achieve." Stop right now and reread that quote, let it sink in.

I want you to understand that if you have a goal, a dream or desire to achieve anything in life, you can make it happen. It will take hard work, there's no doubt about that. But in the end, the hard work is what makes actually reaching your goals worth it. So here's what you need to do when you want to dream big and achieve any goals (Mind you I'm still learning this and working on it myself):

1. Define your goal - Be specific about what you want such as a beautiful lake front home with mountain views.
2. Let it set in - Begin to truly believe that you can achieve this goal, don't worry about how you'll get there, we'll discuss that in a second. You're going to recite your goal daily.
3. Begin to devise your plan - Think about how you're going to achieve your goal - what can you do to make it a reality. Break it down piece by piece and it becomes easier and easier to achieve.
4. Get to work. Start pushing yourself to accomplish things bit by bit.
5. Keep working! This is the hardest part for me. I'm an expert at starting projects or coming up with grandiose plans, but I have a hard time sticking with them.
6. Document your progress and celebrate breakthroughs. Remember to keep yourself motivated and celebrate milestones, it'll make the journey more fun.

That's it. That's a simple method to finding your success and accomplishing anything you think about. And that's why I believe in you. Because now you have access to a simple and easy to follow plan that can truly change your life and the lives of those around you. Trust me. It's beginning to work for me, and I'm confident the future is going to hold some amazing things for our family because of it.

The Meaning of Life

Life is a complicated thing, we're put in this place with millions of things to learn and experience in our short time here, but no real guide book on how to do it. So we all search and stumble our way through it as best we can, hopefully learning more from those that came before us. A big part of the reason we're here is to work through our weaknesses to become better and better as we go. I like to think of it as leveling up.

As I've grown up, I've been able to pick up on a lot of my weaknesses and actually do something about them. Things like the fact that I'm incredibly impatient -- I hate waiting for things, I'm not the most confident person in the world, or my shyness. I've been able to find work arounds for many of these things and I'm in the process of conquering them altogether.

You should do the same in your life, find the areas that you can improve upon and devote yourself to becoming the absolute best you can. It's through these changes that we grow and we learn the most in life. To keep it simple, push yourself, grow and help others along the way.

....

"The meaning of life is that it is to be lived, and it is not to be traded and conceptualized and squeezed into a pattern of systems."
- Bruce Lee
....

The World Is Full Of Good People

I want to tell you that the world is filled with a lot more good people than bad, despite what the news tells you. They have an end product in mind - selling advertising. And what draws people in to watch their shows and read their websites? Drama - whether it's violence or someone doing something bad, those ideas captivate people's minds. I know for a fact, because I'm just as susceptible. I love seeing destruction and mayhem, that's why I'm a fire fighter. But I get a hell of a lot better feeling when I can talk with the homeowners whose dog I rescued or fire I put out. Those connections and knowing you truly helped someone in need are the real value.

  I was at a chimney fire once, it was brutally cold out, snow on the ground and we were working like crazy to reach their chimney because it was an odd house set up. I took a moment to talk to the homeowners about getting their dog to a warm spot, and you couldn't believe how much that meant to them that even though there were a hundred other things going on, someone showed them compassion and wanted to help keep their dog warm.

  That's what It's like to be a good person. And they responded appropriately sending a thank you letter to the fire house and mentioning that one moment out of all the other stuff that was going on.

  The vast majority of people you'll encounter as you work your way through life will be willing to help you out. The only problem I see is that because of the internet and how fast ideas spread now, our society is getting conditioned to expect that strangers are all evil. I just wanted to tell you that they aren't. Seriously, just try saying 'Hi' to a random person as you're out walking or doing some shopping. It will surprise the hell out of them, but I bet they say "Hi' back.

Wisdom

....
"No man was ever wise by chance" - Seneca
....

Gaining wisdom in your life will come from experiencing life, learning as much as you can and by failing. Each of these moments will help you grow and become the person you are meant to be in their own way. Wisdom is not something that can be simply learned through classes or reading, to truly understand it, it must be seen, heard, and felt.

You Don't Know Everything

I've been fortunate most of my life. I've never been the type of person that thought I knew everything. In fact, I was always willing to listen. That's a very valuable lesson.

There will be times in your life where you think you know everything there is to know about a subject or a skill that needs to be done, and yet someone else will try to teach you or explain a different way. Unless your life is in immediate danger and you know your skill will save you, take a moment and listen to them.

That insight that they give to you may be valuable, it may not, but it will do a few key things for you.

1. It will establish to the other person that you're not a know it all, you value other people's thoughts, insights and ideas. That creates an instant likeability with you.
2. You'll gain a new perspective - everyone looks at things and does them differently, their way could be a lot better and faster than the one you already know.

You'll undoubtedly face moments in your life, I'm sure many will be when you're listening to me or your mother talk to you about something. Rather than tuning us out and not paying attention, perk up, take in our perspective and engage us in a rational conversation. We will always listen to your input, you may be wrong, because we're your parents and we're always right, but we'll always give you an opportunity to voice your side of things.

And who knows, maybe we'll learn a few things from you too. You've already taught us so much in the 2 years we've been graced with your presence, so I'm excited to see how much more you can teach me in the future.

Live On Purpose

Live a purpose driven life. Everyone needs a purpose, a reason to get up every day and put in the hard work. It's easy to be stagnant if you're lacking purpose, to never push yourself out of your comfort zones and to try and achieve what they say is impossible. There's no greater power than to wake up every day with a clearly defined purpose to fulfill. When you narrow down your purpose, and you're truly passionate about what you're working towards, you'll be far more fulfilled than the average person.

This Is The Show

This life is the show. It's not the time to continually rehearse, it's time to get out there and live it, perform your life in only the way you can.

Sleep

When you're a kid, naps are overrated. When you're a teenager you'll sleep more than any human could conceive. When you're a young adult, you think you can survive on 3 hours of sleep after a raging party. When you have young kids you will survive on broken sleep. Beyond that age... well, I'll just have to wait and see how sleep pans out.

Getting the right amount of sleep, under the right conditions is essential. It makes you happier, and more ready to take on the day. If you're constantly tired, you'll never be able to achieve your full potential. You can take as much caffeine as you want, but your mind will never be in a peak state. I've experienced far too many sleepless nights in my life, and there's nothing your body needs more than to be able to have a steady sleep schedule, it really is an essential part of being alive.

Take Chances

A war was never won, a mission never achieved, a life never well lived from someone who didn't take chances. Put yourself out there, follow your dreams and try new things. A life is only worth living if you're fully living it.

Those who sit and wait for the world to produce results for them will never truly understand the power of taking a chance on your dreams and the power that comes with that.

Laugh

Life is a serious thing, but if you can't laugh along the way, it just may not be worth living.

Laugh often and be able to laugh at yourself.

Experience Life

Experience everything life has to offer you. Take it all in. It's going to throw challenges your way and put obstacles in your path, but you can get beyond those. Get outside of your comfort zone and see what new experiences you can encounter.

This world is filled with so many amazing things, awesome people and incredible opportunities. You have the ability to choose anything you want to pursue.

For as long as I can remember, I've been obsessed with nature, being in amazing places and taking in the sights, sounds and smells. It's an incredibly powerful feeling to be exploring the things that get you most excited in this life.

You should have that too. You should wake up to the world everyday excited to learn, explore and do amazing things. It won't always be an easy task to pursue, but I can guarantee you it will always be worth it.

Explore Your Faith

Explore your faith. We're not a very religious family, so that will never be pushed on you. But I want to encourage you to learn about different religions and belief systems. Maybe you'll find something in one of them that resonates with you. That's not to say you have to convert entirely to a religion, but merely take bits and pieces that fit with your beliefs and use them to guide you in your life's mission.

....

"Just as a candle cannot burn without fire, men cannot live without a spiritual life." - Buddha

....

Know What You Want

Know what you want out of life. I know, it's not as easy as that. You don't have to know the entire big picture of what you think your life will be like, but know what you want in the moment and near future so you can discipline yourself to take the right actions to reach your goals. If you have no idea what you want, you're far more likely to be swayed towards the things you don't want or shouldn't be involved in.

And in those moments of your life where you feel totally lost, know how to get yourself back to a grounded position.

Everything You've Got

Everything you've got. The world demands that you give everything you've got to make your dreams a reality. Push yourself harder and further each and every day. Ordinary people will stop pushing themselves when they get comfortable.

Don't let that be you. Keep going. Keep giving and keep working towards bigger and better things. Not a single one of the world's most successful or inspirational people ever said "That's enough, I can stop pursuing my goals now." And neither can you. Just strike those statements from your mind because if you're going to fulfill your dreams, you're going to have to work harder, smarter and longer than ordinary people. But I promise you, the end result will be worth it every time.

One Life

We all have one life to live, one lifetime to give, to serve, to help and to make a difference in this world. Don't squander your one opportunity to do something amazing.

The Stars

The stars rise and fall just as your life experiences will. You'll have those moments where you don't think things could get much worse, and before you know it, you're whisked up to the greatest moments you've ever experienced. Understand that life happens in cycles, but your response to each of these moments will determine how long the cycles last and how great they are.

Watch The Clouds

Watch the clouds as they shift and change. Life is all about constant and never ending change.

There will be changes that you don't care for, changes that you've been waiting an eternity for, and there will be changes that you've worked so incredibly hard to achieve. It's important to know that changes will happen whether you want them to or not just as the clouds change their shape, speed and density throughout the day.

Embrace these changes as best you can, understand that one change leads to another and another, eventually putting you right where you want to be the most.

Don't Fear Hard Work

Don't fear hard work, it's far more rewarding than taking the easy route. When you begin to expect life to hand you everything you want without the work, you're setting yourself up for failure. The world isn't going to just simply hand over everything you want. You will have to work for it. Your achievements will be that much better when you've invested in yourself to achieve them.

Don't Live Each Day As Though It Were Your Last

There's a very common phrase that says something to the effect of "live each day as though it's your last." I think that's flawed, and incredibly so. If today were my last day alive, I wouldn't do 90% of the things I'm doing each day. And you might challenge me with "Then why are you doing those things?" It's simple. I need to make a living, I need to provide for you, build wealth and look towards the future. And I can't do those things if I were focused on living my life like it were my very last day to be alive.

Now I do agree with implementing elements of what I would do if it were my last day, like spending time with you, my family or friends and having great experiences. But there's no way you can possibly make the life you want to live if you are forever focused on living like it were your last day alive. Unfortunately we never know exactly when our time will be up, so don't focus on when it will end, instead, focus on building the life you want to live today and in the future.

Be Yourself

There is nobody quite like you on this planet, that's what makes meeting new people so interesting. Don't be afraid to be who you truly are. Imitating others will only get you so far, and you'll feel like a fraud in the process.

Express yourself. Do the things you love to do. Be with the people you want to be around. Imagine your own dreams, not those of others around you. Be uniquely you, and nobody can compete with that.

You'll draw more people in when they can sense your genuine personality and they know they're talking to the real you.

....
"If you are always trying to be normal, you will never know how amazing you can be." - Maya Angelou
....

In your relationships, be yourself. Don't pretend to be someone you're not, that's the surest way to set your relationship up for failure. Be open. Be honest. And be you. If they can't fall in love with the real you, it may not be meant to be.

Your Past
Everyone has a past. That's a given. And your past represents a lot about who you were in those moments. But your past does not dictate where you decide to take your life in the future. You have the ability to create the future you want. So don't look to your past to determine your future life. Just because your life was one way doesn't mean it has to continue down that path if you don't want it to.

Problems
Problems will arise in your life, the key is all in how you respond to those problems. Do you sit back and let the world happen to you? Or do you go out and find solutions and overcome those obstacles? The latter is always the better answer.

Those that sit back and expect the world to solve their problems will never make anything of themselves. They will never contribute and leave the world a better place than when they arrived if they constantly remain in that state. And that's really the core of why we're all here; to leave the world a better place, even if it's just ever so slightly.

There Will Be Struggles

There will be moments in your life where you will struggle. You will fight and claw with everything you have to get to a better place. Trust in yourself. Know that your perseverance and determination will get you through those struggles. Pay attention during these struggles and you'll learn invaluable lessons.

It's Your Responsibility

It's your responsibility to choose the direction of your life. Nobody else can do that for you. If you're sitting there waiting for it to happen, you're going to fall into someone's else grand plan, and that's not something you should allow to happen. I've sat idly by expecting these great things to come my way at certain points of my life, and they never came. Instead, I found myself chugging along a path that was no longer what I desired. You can avoid that by taking responsibility and putting in the effort to make your life what you want it to be.

Live With A Sense Of Wonder

Live your life with a sense of wonder and excitement. Never let the little things pass you by without noticing them. Let your curiosity guide you towards new and amazing things. As much as we would love to think we're the supreme beings, not a single thing we have could exist without the interaction of the rest of the world. Everything from the tiny worms and caterpillars to the giant grizzly bears, they all play a role in making the earth and our lives what they really are.

....

"We are shaped by our thoughts; we become what we think. When the mind pure, joy follows like a shadow that never leaves." - Buddha

....

Help Others

We were all put here for a purpose. What that entire purpose is, I have no idea, I don't think anyone does, though many will claim they do. What I do know is that we should always be looking for ways to help other people. How you choose to help those people is really up to you, because there are literally thousands of ways you could go about doing that. You can help people emotionally, physically, mentally, strategically, you get the idea. Find ways you can help other people and the universe will reward you.

Your Mind

Your mind is awesome. It's a place you can escape to, you can grow from, you can access for knowledge and you can tap into emotions. You hold a lot of power in your mind, use it appropriately.

Validation

We all seek validation in our lives. We want to feel like we're right, we're doing the correct thing, or people appreciate the things we do. It's ok to have those feelings, but I want you to know that you don't NEED them in order to follow your dreams. You don't need people to accept your ideas publicly or to say it's ok, you know in your mind what's right, follow that.

Waiting for validation from other people is like waiting for a blizzard in the middle of summer. The odds of it happening are slim, and completely unnecessary in the first place. Instead of waiting for validation, get started, take action and people will validate it when they see the results. The beautiful part is that when you get the results you were looking for, you don't need their validation.

There Is A Rhythm To Life

There is a very distinct rhythm to everyone's life. But the beauty of it is something very few people realize, and thus very few people take advantage of. You can control your rhythm just the same way a composer does. You see people walking around hitting peaks and valleys every single day. When you learn how to control your thoughts and control your mind, you can keep yourself out of those valleys and stay on level ground or up the beautiful mountain peaks. The choice is yours.

Family Is Like A Spider Web

Your family is like a spider web. You may not interact with every member or strand of the web at all times, but lose one or two and the whole thing can come crashing down. I don't want you to use that as an excuse to rely on your family for everything, but to understand that they are there as a massive support network for you. Treat them well, take care of them and help them prosper and they'll do the same for you.

The Little Things Do Matter

I laid down to rest in anticipation of a 12 hour shift at the 911 center, when I came downstairs afterwards, Ben was playing with some trucks and gave me a huge hug. Matt was playing in the toy box, saw Ben and I, said "Da" and came crawling over to see me.

I started writing down daily gratitude a little over a year and a half ago. I keep it simple, 3-5 things that I'm thankful for every day. Sometimes they're things I've experienced, or the people in my life, or even just having awesome weather. It doesn't matter what I write down, as long as it's something I appreciate and it's positive.

It's an incredibly powerful habit that you can start doing immediately to change the way you think and perceive things on a daily basis. Instead of always focusing on the negative, you can focus your thoughts on looking for the positive things in life.

Daily gratitude forced a radical change in my mindset, and if you're not doing it, I would highly suggest you try it. Not just for a day or two. Make a serious and committed effort to do it for at least a month. Pay attention in the moment and be thankful for all the awesome things that come your way.

Fast Forward Theory

When you're young, life never seems like it's moving fast enough. You can't wait till next week to go on vacation or to another party. The summer seems like it lasts forever. Appreciate that, because it won't seem that way forever.

At certain points in your life, it seems like someone hits a fast forward button. Time seems to speed up. Your mind is so full of information, and you have more of your time committed to things you may not enjoy doing. For me, it was right after High School that the button was hit for the first time. I got my first full time job and started going to school full time simultaneously. Life got hectic and filled quickly. I lost focus on what really mattered most to me, my friends, my family and having fun.

The world has a funny way of filling itself to the max and taking over your life. It's up to you to slow it down, control your thoughts and where you dedicate your energy to make sure you're living the life you want to experience.

Over the course of my life since getting out of school, that fast forward button has been hit several times. I've worked to slow it down as much as possible. But you should realize, being an adult requires a whole lot more from you than being a kid, so take it in, experience everything you can experience and love being young. Make sure you appreciate life as you experience it.

That's not to say there aren't advantages of being an adult. If you engineer your life properly, you'll have more freedom, you can buy the things you want and go where ever you want to. But it's up to you to make that happen. Live your life at 1x, not 16x, it's the only way to make sure you get everything out of life that you want.

Don't let your days get filled to the brim with useless thoughts, inaction or fear. Take control and live the life you want to live.

Safety

We all crave the feeling of being safe. To never have to worry. It's comfortable. It's a natural state to seek out. That's why so many people stay stuck in one place forever. It's comfortable, it's safe and it provides all the basics they require. But to really grow, you'll have to put yourself into a vulnerable state. You'll have to expose yourself to the chaos of the world.

There's plenty of ways to do that calculated so you can minimize risk, but if you're seeking ways to break free from the ordinary, to be extraordinary, there's no way to stay in that safe zone forever. It could be as simple as speaking up, or more complex like literally fighting to save lives, whatever it may be, know that true, unlimited growth happens when we break out of the safety zone we're all used to.

Weakness

We all have weaknesses in our lives. No matter how big and powerful you become, you will always have a weakness. The key to handling those is to recognize that they exist, and then find ways to strengthen them. Now that of course means something else may shift to become your new weakness. Follow that same path for the new weakness, and before you know it you'll be in an incredible upward climb towards greatness.

Freedom

You have the freedom to live the life you want to. Take full advantage of all the opportunities around you. Follow your inquisitive nature. Explore things that fascinate you. These are the very things that will lead you to your passion in life.

If You Sincerely Want To Change...

If you sincerely want to change your life, you have no choice but to open yourself up to new ideas. You'll have to put yourself outside of your comfort zone, to challenge your personal status quo, to invigorate your soul to reach a higher level.

Throughout your life, people will be pushing you to change one way, and then another. Listen only to those changes that make sense deep down within you. Don't blindly follow the paths of others. Their journey towards change and growth may be entirely different than yours is intended to be.

Sometimes in life, we need to get off the well-worn trail, and blaze our own path to find our true reason for being.

Feeling Alive

To feel fully alive... It's something we all strive for. And yet, we often find ourselves over burdened, under motivated and stressed. We praise technology as this great thing, and yet we've all become slaves to it. To feel fully alive, you must break free from it, get back to the basics of life. Simplify your life. Reduce the number of inputs coming your way. Get back to real world experiences that will leave a lasting impact on you and your imagination.

It's All Limited

"Remembering that I'll be dead soon is the most important tool I've ever encountered to help me make the big choices in life. Because almost everything - all external expectations, all pride, all fear of embarrassment or failure - these things just fall away in the face of death, leaving only what is truly important." - Steve Jobs

Pay Attention To The World Around You

Pay attention to the world around you. We live in a crazy, over developed, ever evolving world. Things change at lightning speed, and it's only going to get faster as the decades roll on. Because of that, it's important that you pay attention. You must understand, at least at the core, everything that is happening in the world.

There's no way you could possibly take in everything you're going to need to succeed in this world by merely reading. Observe people and their actions. Watch their emotions. Take it all in. You'll learn so many more things when you actually slow down and consume everything the world has to show you.

And while I want to encourage you to pay attention to the world, I also want to caution you against making it an obsession. You have a life, you have goals, passions and people that are important to you, make sure you continue to invest your time and energy into those things.

Have Strong Principles

It's important for you to stand for something in your life. Life is crazy. It will always be that way. But you can make a lot more sense of it when you have simple, yet strong guiding principles to follow.

Your principles create a foundation for you to build from. And that foundation is really the core of who you are. Remain open to new thoughts and ideas, and be ready to remove part of your core and replace it with more relevant pieces from time to time, but no matter what you do, have a clearly defined foundation for your life. For me, those things are honesty, giving back (volunteering and donating), helping others prosper and protecting nature.

We All Have An Innocence About Us

I had an incredibly stress filled day. I was exhausted. Stressed from kids jumping all over me. Lost on how to move towards a better life. I wasn't happy. And then, as I lay on the couch trying to relax, I witnessed Ben sitting there at the table, doing nothing more than eating. At 2, like most meals, it was more of a task than simply eating, but it was as though I awoke to reality.

No matter how stressed I am, no matter what's going on in the world around me, this boy is filled with pure innocence. At 2, he aims to do nothing more than enjoy his time and please Mommy and Daddy. He wants to be filled with pride, to experience only good times and to grow up to be just like his parents. He knows of nearly no evils. They simply don't exist in his mind, and there is no place for them there. I don't want to squander these days.

Have you ever had one of those moments when someone stresses you out so much or gets you so incredibly angry that you're just filled with despise for them? And then, in your angered state, you witness them doing the most mundane of human things like making a meal, doing yard work, or watching tv. And then it hits you. Whatever crap you were feeling towards them was nothing more than pure emotions. You realize they're just as lost, confused and emotionally drained as you are. You can't help but bring yourself back to reality and let your issues go.

Part Two:
Being Human

Welcome To Life, Being Human Isn't Easy...

Being human is about the common traits we all face. Growing up, we're all confronted with similar problems, and yes, some people will face them with a silver spoon in their mouth, others will face them while battling poverty. That's just a fact of life. But the problems at their core are all still the same, no matter what type of life you're brought into.

The trouble I see in the world is that so many people don't understand the power they hold, the ability they have to change their own lives and to lead the lifestyle they want. But more importantly to change others' lives too. At the time I'm publishing this, I've been the same way for most of my life. It's only in the last few years (2012 - 2014) that I began to truly understand how I am the only one responsible for the life I lead.

For most of us, we no longer live in a society where you are told what you will become, and bucking that trend is career suicide. No one can dictate what you will become in this life, and I feel that will become ever more prevalent as you come into adulthood.

Right now, I'm sitting at the cusp of a revolution. A revolution where people are leaving the traditional job system and creating the lives they want to live. We lost the sense of security when major companies began laying off tens of thousands of people and haven't stopped. I'm not saying you need to grind out your own path in life, it's perfectly fine to work for someone else, but remember, it's an option, not a necessity to do so.

As you grow up, you're going to be faced with stress, the need to make sacrifices, opinions and questions of faith. This part simply aims to help guide you through these moments in your life.

Anger Is Natural

I'm not just saying that to have a cop out for the moments when my frustration gets the better of me. It's true. It's a natural emotion we all have deep inside of us. For some people, it pops up more often and in greater quantities, but we all have it. I for one have very little patience, I get frustrated when I have to wait for things, which is why I will avoid certain activities or plan them in a way that I won't have to wait long.

Listen; there are a lot of things in life that will drive you up a wall. And I'm writing this to tell you that it's ok. Its life and things will happen that you don't like. What really matters is how you deal with it.

Find methods to vent, relax and get your anger out in a helpful way. Doing that will keep you in control of your mind, your emotions and where you're heading in life.

....

"Remember that stress doesn't come from what's going on in your life. It comes from your thoughts about what's going on in your life." - Andrew Bernstein

....

Life Is Sometimes Unpleasant

In life, there are often times where things don't go as planned. It may be painful, or perhaps frustrating. But it's in these times where we're challenged that we grow the most. So go forward, keep on pushing when you hit unpleasant times. Each and every lesson we tackle becomes knowledge, and that knowledge gives us a lot of potential power.

One thing I've learned is that we're often presented with a lesson that for whatever reason (god, spirit, nature) has determined we need to tackle. If we fail to invest our time and energy in overcoming these things and learning the lessons when they arise, and instead choose to sit back and wait for normalcy to return, we will have to face these lessons again. They will continue to show up until we choose to take control of them and turn them into an asset instead of a liability.

Mistakes In Love

Making mistakes in love and relationships are going to be some of your most painful mistakes. In fact, loving someone can be one of the most painful things you do at times. That's not to say you should never fall in love or be in a serious relationship, because you'd be missing out on some of life's best things too. But when you're in a serious relationship, you're giving up a large part of yourself and trusting another person not to hurt you.

Most of the time, that will work out great. They will respect you, love you and be there to back you up along your journey in life. But you need to be prepared that things may not always pan out how you had hoped.

I had a longtime girlfriend that I met when I was 16. We dated well into college and I was head over heels for this girl. When people say they would give their life for someone, that's quite often bull, but this, well this was serious. If a moment had presented itself where I needed to make a life or death decision then, I would have surely sacrificed my life for her.

But our relationship wasn't all glitz and glamour. We had our ups and downs like any relationship, and the more that I look back on things now, the more I realize the number of mistakes I made. Many were just me being me and needing to learn who I really was, but those things also had a huge impact on the quality of our relationship.

There's no sugar coating things. I used to be as lazy as a sloth. I would seize any shortcut I could, and was never super motivated to do much with my life. I wasn't the type of guy that was just sitting at home eating Doritos and playing video games all day, but I should have been more active and more inspired. After high school, I was working full time and going to college full time.

But I wasn't devoting the right amount of time to continuing to build my relationship with this girl. I assumed that the relationship was good and things would take care of themselves. And because of that, we began to grow apart. As time went on, we had the typical arguments so many couples have, and she eventually had enough of it.

She decided to move on in life, and I was completely devastated. In all honesty, this was the absolute hardest moment I had in my life up until that point. I brought myself down, and dragged myself through hell. I won't get into the details of that time period, because that's not what"s important at the moment, but I do think it's important for you to realize, especially as you get older, that almost everyone will go through heartbreak and rough times in a relationship.

It took me a long time to get over her. And I'd be lying if I didn't tell you that I still think about her from time to time, but it's in a good way. I use it as a sense of reflection on where I once was, the things I screwed up on, and how I can really use that to my advantage to prevent those same mistakes in future relationships.

Some advice:

- Don't be selfish - A relationship is about a lot more than just yourself and your desires.
- Listen - I mean this in all sincerity. Shut off your outside thinking, and listen to the other person. Pay attention to their thoughts, what scares them, what makes them happy and what they want in a relationship.
- Use those things to make their life better - If you can make them happy, do it. If you can help them think through their problems, do it. It's not complicated, just be a good person and this will come easier than you think.
- Be willing to sacrifice - I was always a home body, she wanted to go out, but we rarely did. That really hurt our relationship. Be willing to step out of your comfort zone so the other person can enjoy their life too. You should both be willing to sacrifice for one another.
- Share experiences - Make sure you get out and enjoy life. There's too many amazing things to see in this world to spend all of your time watching reruns on tv. Get outside and try something new with them.

People Will Come And Go From Your Life

No matter where you choose to go in life, or what you choose to be, people will be a constant. Unless you decide to go live in the middle of the woods without anyone around, you'll always have people around you. Some will stay for the long run, others will enter your life only for a short time.

There's no reason to be sad for those that choose not to stay long, they're on their own journey in life. Take the lessons and joys that they give to you and harness those to grow yourself and make your life better each and every day.

Remember, everybody will serve a purpose in the bigger picture of your life, even if it's not immediately apparent at the time. I've been heartbroken and lost, forced to work my way through, and even though it wasn't easy, I always came out better for having done that. Life isn't always easy or fair, but there is always something that can be learned from others.

There's a quote that I saw once, and I love it. I don't recall the words exactly or who said it, but it went something like this. "Remember, we're all just an extra in someone else's movie."

That's powerful, and when you stop to think about the real meaning in that, it should be humbling to you. You're not the center of the world, in fact, you're a tiny tiny piece of it all. Everyone else is wandering just as aimlessly, as lost and confused about their next step in life as you are.

And when you pass that person on the street that you normally wouldn't give another glance to, instead, remember, you're just an extra in their movie, but if you make an impression on them, you can suddenly become a leading role.

....

"You don't know what people are really like until they're under a lot of stress." - Tim Allen

....

Take Time To Help Others

I've spent my entire adult life dedicating it to helping others. It's not always fun, and it's certainly not easy, but it does have its upsides.

I can't tell you exactly how many lives I've helped to save in some role, but I know it's a lot. I don't say that to gloat, but because I'm proud of what I've done. I know that I've been able to help people in the worst moments of their lives, and many times with positive outcomes.

You don't need to get into public safety like your mother and I, but I do implore you to take the time to help others in any way you can. Be it simply passing off a dollar to a stranger in need, lending an ear to a good friend, or volunteering your time for an organization that strikes your heart.

There's probably no greater thing you can do in this life than to take the time to help others.

Insecurities

We all experience insecurities in our life. We think we're too fat, too inexperienced, too old, too young, too poor, too ugly. You name it and someone at some point has thought it. Everyone has some sort of insecurities in their lifetime. If you're going to achieve great things in your life, you need to move beyond them.

These insecurities serve you no purpose other than to limit your life and your potential for success. Remember, they're all just part of a mindset, a mindset that you can choose to change at any point.

Stress

Life is full of stressful moments. Some will challenge you mentally, others physically but the end result is all the same, your mind and your body feel the effects. The key is whether you allow your mind and body to feel the full impact. What do I mean by that?

Take control of your thoughts. If you're feeling stressed, focus on creating a way to alleviate the stress, and best of all, a way that the stress doesn't impact your life again. Don't shy away and let it overcome you.

....

"The greatest weapon against stress is our ability to choose one thought over another."
– William James

....

Take Responsibility

Take responsibility for your life. You're the only one that can hold you accountable for the things you do and what you want out of life. So be a responsible person, accept that you are the only person that can make your life what you want it to be, and then get started making that happen.

....

"No one saves us but ourselves. No one can and no one may. We ourselves must walk the path."
– Buddha

....

Don't Regret What You've Done

Don't regret what you've done in your life. Maybe you didn't follow through on something you said you would. Or maybe you wished you had handled something differently. Whatever the case may be, it's in the past. There's no sense in dwelling on it now. You have the ability to move your life forward in any direction you choose. Don't let your past hold you back from doing that.

Everything you did in the past represents where your thoughts and actions were at the time. Learn from those moments and use them to help you grow into a better and more inspiring leader.

Honesty

....
"A man can only be trusted as much as his word."
- Chris Lockwood
....

You must always be honest. This isn't something you can bargain with or dabble in. When you lack honesty, you lack integrity. Without integrity you lose trust and that begins a slippery slope.

The most trusted people in the world are the most honest. When honesty is lost, it cannot be regained.

Comfort Zone

I've suffered in comfort zones for a long time. It's way too easy to sit in them and get nothing accomplished. Comfort zones suck. While you feel all warm and cuddly, they limit your ability to grow as a person, to push yourself to new levels. We should spend our lives trying to avoid these comfort zones rather than seeking them out. By doing that we can constantly remain in a state of personal growth.

Sacrifices

Sacrifice now for future gain. You have dreams that you want to achieve right? And to reach those dreams there's no way you can continue doing all the things you want to do. You can't watch tv all day and eat fast food if you want to have an amazing body, those two things don't mesh. So if that were your case, you'd have to sacrifice tv and fast food for more amazing food and being active, doing something you enjoy doing.

Sacrifice for someone else's gain. I've sacrificed a lot in my life for other people. I've done things I really didn't want to do, like helping someone move or going to party I didn't want to attend. I did these things not for myself, but to help my friends and family progress in their lives and to support them. That's important. You wield so much more power when you can help move others forward in their lives instead of always thinking about yourself. Balance this delicately though, there are times you need to say no, you can't give up your entire life for other people if you have your own goals and objectives.

Small sacrifices can lead to incredible gains. You don't always have to make massive sacrifices in your life to see the changes happen that you're looking for. Often a single tweak to your life can catapult you into the zone you're looking for. You may be sitting on the edge of success and one small change or sacrifice could get you over that edge.

Accept Your Emotions

We all have emotions appear in our lives. Maybe you're frustrated, tired, happy or mad. It doesn't matter what it is, accept what you're feeling and determine whether that's going to benefit you or hurt you. Then base your actions on that solid ground, not your emotional state.

Be Consistent

Be consistent. The worst type of person is one that can't predict their own actions and thoughts. Play the game of life in the most consistent manner you can. Create a life that you're proud of and that others can rely on.

I've had a lot of friends over the years that I could never predict what they were going to do, even when they gave me their word. As you can likely tell now, they are no longer a part of my life because I couldn't count on them. Don't let yourself become that person.

Reliable

Be a reliable person. When you make promises, keep them. Show up when you say you will. Follow through on actions you promise you'll make. Be that person the world can trust to get things done. Don't give people the opportunity to ever second guess you or your word.

Forgiveness

I've always been able to let things go pretty quickly, that is unless you really hurt me. It's important to remember that everybody makes mistakes, they make judgment calls that may be good for them and hurtful for you. They're learning, growing and experiencing life just as much as you are. Most of life's mistakes can be forgiven when you remember they're just as lost and confused as you are.

....

"The weak can never forgive. Forgiveness is the attribute of the strong." - Mahatma Gandhi

"To err is human; to forgive, divine" - Alexander Pope

....

Handling Change

There will be a lot of changes that happen in your life. If you're anything like me, changes won't be the easiest thing you deal with. That's ok. There's a challenge in them that we need to face to move on to the next stage in our lives. The simplest advice I have about changes is to try and embrace them as best you can, take an optimistic outlook about what the future will look like and power on.

....

"In times of great stress or adversity, it's always best to keep busy, to plow your anger and your energy into something positive." - Lee Iacocca

....

Trust Your Gut

Trust your gut, it's usually right. I can't tell you the number of times I've gone against my gut reaction and been completely wrong. I've learned to trust my instincts more than the rationalizing I try to do in my mind.

There's something magical about the way your instincts work. You'll know that feeling when it hits you. Follow it. Don't let your mind wander or draw you towards other options, they're typically the wrong ones. The universe sends you signals, act on them.

Being Brave

Being brave isn't so much about running into burning buildings and rescuing people. That does take a lot of bravery to do, but there are so many more moments in your life where bravery will come into play than those big incidents. Being brave could mean facing your own irrational fears, overcoming an obstacle or remaining strong when other people are trying to bring you down. Those are the real moments where your bravery can shine and in reality will make the biggest difference in both your life and the lives of others.

Fighting Your Monsters

No, not the big green and blue ones with massive teeth that sneak in to your bedroom through your closet to scare you. I'm talking about the kind of monsters that cause you to limit yourself. The kind that make you second guess what you're about to do because you're irrationally afraid of what may happen. I have always defined myself as a fairly shy person, but over the years, I've pushed myself to work through that and intentionally gone out of my way to talk to people or introduce myself when I could have just as easily walked by them. It's about finding your irrational fears and then intentionally working on them so you overcome them and they no longer hold you back.

Connect With People

Connect with people on a deeper level, have the kind of conversations that make you feel vulnerable. Not with everyone of course, but with certain select people that will help you grow as a person, and you can do the same for them.

Help Others

Life is not just about living and growing yourself. That's a good place to start, but it's short lived if you never put those skills to good use helping other people. Your mother and I have devoted a larger portion of our lives to public safety and helping people in many of the worst moments of their lives as firefighters, emt's, police officers and dispatchers.

That is how we have chosen to help people, at least in this phase of our lives. I implore you to find a way to help others that feels natural to you, perhaps it's the same way we do, or something entirely different, the method doesn't matter so much as the action you take. The end goal really is just to go out of your own way and to put other people's needs before your own.

Don't Be In A Rush To Grow Up

As a kid, it seems like getting older can't happen soon enough. You're constantly in awe of all the things adults do like driving a car, going anywhere they want when they want, having money to buy things, etc. Don't be in a rush to grow up. You have plenty of time in your life to work and be an adult. You only get to be a kid once, and having an awesome childhood is one of the greatest gifts I can give to you.

I don't regret growing up fast, it was just the way things landed on my plate. I bear witness to many things that I will never forget when I was just a kid and joined the fire department. I feel like I was prepared for them, but in reality, you can never be fully prepared for all of the chaos of life. They don't plague my mind, but they certainly weren't a necessary part of my childhood growth.

Enjoy your youth, it will seem like it goes on forever, but one day you'll look back only to reminisce about the good times you had. Make sure you enjoy those good times and live every single day in a way you would love to look back on. My parents gave me a great childhood, and I plan to do the same for you.

Turn The Bad Into Good

You have ability to turn every bad thing into something good. For starters, what you perceive as bad, is just that, a perception of your mind's creation. Everything that happens in life just is what it is, it only means something when we give it the right to in our mind. So even a tragedy doesn't have to be a 'bad' thing if you don't want it to be, don't let it take hold in your mind in that way.

For that to work, you also need to understand that there are lessons to be learned from everything that happens to you in life. Tragedies will happen, lovers will leave you, people will die, that's all just a part of living and being alive. That's not to say those times aren't difficult to work through, but they become ever more valuable when you realize the lesson being taught to you. Often it's as simple as being able to appreciate what you had, and sometimes it's more complicated and requires deep thought.

The world is a crazy, weird yet beautiful place. Remember, you're on a journey here to improve yourself and to work on goals you need to get through. Take the lessons as they come to you, and learn all you can from them, because when you try to dismiss them or ignore them, they will eventually come back to you and you'll have to face them all over again.

Take the things you perceive as bad, find the lesson in them and appreciate it for what it is. You have the power to perceive anything in any way you want to, but remember, it's far better to live a happy life and to understand the problems you've encountered than to just dismiss them.

....

"Sometimes when people are under stress, they hate to think, and it's the time when they most need to think."
– William J. Clinton

....

Be Active

Be active. It doesn't really matter what you're doing, but get up and do something. You'll feel better, get more done and stay in better shape without having to exercise all that often. I've lost months of my life sitting in front of the TV mindlessly watching whatever came up with the flip of the channel. I wish I could get that time back, but I can't, so don't let that happen to you. Get outside, live your life and create experiences with your friends, you'll be glad you did.

Tell The Truth

> "If you tell the truth, you don't have to remember anything."
> – Mark Twain

There may be pain in telling the truth, but it's better to face that pain head on than to twist yourself into a tangle of lies that will hurt far more in the future. Lying will get you nowhere fast. I've always been an incredibly honest person, it's just a part of who I am, and hopefully you're the same way. If you're not though, know that every lie you tell takes away from a certain level of trust you've built up. And if no one can trust you, you'll quickly find yourself with few friends.

> "No man has a good enough memory to be a successful liar."
> – Abraham Lincoln

Always Do What's Right

> "Always do what is right. It will gratify half of mankind and astound the other."
> – Mark Twain

The right thing is not always the easiest thing to do. In fact, it's quite often the harder thing to do. But if you set out to do the right thing up front, it makes your life far better in the long run.

> "Control and Responsibility are the SAME THING. If you want control over something, you must take responsibility for it. You have FAR more power than you know." - Jesse Elder

Opinions

Everyone has their opinions. Some people love to share them more than others, but everyone has them. An opinion is just that, an opinion. Unless you can provide value and insight into what someone's going through because you have the experience or knowledge, sometimes it's best to keep quiet. Often they aren't looking for your opinion, they're simply venting to get their feelings out.

When you're asked for your opinion, choose your words carefully. There's a lot of power in swaying someone with your opinions and what you think is best, but you probably won't have the full picture of where they're coming from and what they ultimately want in their own life.

You'll gather your views and your opinions on the world from what you see, feel, hear and experience. That's just one aspect of the world though. Your opinion is simply your point of view. Accept that others will have differing opinions at times. It's not that there's always a right or wrong opinion, just merely a different perception based on their life.

Faith

Have faith in yourself and your abilities. You are a powerful human being, and you can change the world in amazing ways. You don't need anyone to affirm that for you other than yourself. Don't let people get inside your head and convince you that you can't do something. Instead, prove them wrong and do miraculous things.

Humble

Being humble is an important skill to learn. I want you to be a strong and powerful person, to get everything you want in life. But I also want you to understand that you're on the same journey as everyone else in this world. There will be times in your life where you'll feel small and inconsequential, remember; there are often bigger things at play in the world than just you. You are important, very important, but you're also just a small piece of the giant puzzle that is earth.

Feel small when you're standing beside mountains. Feel the power of a river as it rushes past you. Feel the serenity of a quiet forest as you sit and contemplate everything life is giving to you. Feel amazed at the power of the human mind. Feel what it's like to give everything you've got towards your goals. Feel what it's like to be empowered beyond your imagination. Feel like you're making a difference in this world, even if it's one teeny tiny thing at a time. Because that one teeny tiny thing could compound and drastically change the world in the best possible ways that you could never imagine.

Remain Calm

I've always been a calm person. It takes a lot to get me worked up, and that's a trait that I cherish. Being able to remain calm even in some of the most stressful moments of your life will help you far more than getting worked up ever could. It allows you to continue to process your thoughts and come up with solutions faster and more accurately than the panic stricken person.

So how do you remain calm?
- Slow your breathing. Become conscious of every breath you take, at least for a few seconds.
- Slow your mind down. You have an overload of information to process, slow it down and take only the core thoughts that need to be dealt with, let the rest go by the wayside.
- Make decisions based solely on those core thoughts or problems.
- Take immediate action if necessary.
- Continue to focus only on the core problems until they're resolved. You can worry about all of the other little details later on.

Practice this as often as you can, that's the only way you'll be able to fully use it when you need it most. Practice during the small moments where you feel yourself getting worked up.

I'll give you a great example from my life. When I was a kid, maybe 8 or 10, we were all at our grandma's house for Christmas day festivities. Aunt Diane was marinating the ham in the oven. When she stood back up and turned around, I noticed she was on fire!

She was wearing a wool sweater that had a snow covered house design on it. As calm as could be, the only comment I could muster out of my mouth was "Uh, Diane, your house is on fire." Maybe it was partly out of naivety that I didn't realize she was literally on fire and the potential for injuries, or just my personality, but I was steadfast in telling her she was on fire in a calm manner. Panic ensued from everyone else around when they realized what was happening, but thankfully they were able to get the fire out quickly and she was uninjured.

You're going to have a lot of moments in your life where it's easy to get worked up and let your emotions take over the situation at hand. Don't let that happen. Practice remaining calm whenever you can. It will help you in so many other ways.

Face What's Holding You Back

There will be times in your life where you're being held back. Surprisingly, I've found that most of what's held me back in life was not outside influences, but rather myself. Even those things that on the surface appear to be outside of your control, are in fact completely within your control to change. Remember, you hold far more power than you realize.

Figure out what's holding you back, and then face those things head on. Tackle them and overcome them so you can live an exceptional life.

Puzzle Pieces

I got this idea from Jesse Elder – a brilliant man. You aren't faced with problems in your life, what you're facing is simply a puzzle that needs to be solved. Don't let yourself get overwhelmed with everything that flows your way, there's a solution, it may take some time to figure out, but there's a solution awaiting you. As you begin to put the puzzle together, it will get easier and easier to figure out where the missing pieces belong.

Freedom

We all strive towards freedom. Freedom to do what we want. Freedom to be friends with who we want. Freedom to live the life we want. But we also limit our own abilities to gain that freedom. We crowd our head with negative thoughts, self-destructive in nature that hold us back from achieving amazing things. Ridding your mind of these thoughts is an essential skill to achieving all the freedoms you wish to possess in your lifetime.

Failure

You will fail at things in life. That's a given. The important thing is to keep getting back up, keep trying, find a way to accomplish the things you want in life. It's easy to sit back, chalk it up on the board as a failure, but it takes a far better man to get up and keep pushing through those failures. The only sure way to achieving the things you want in life is to keep pushing through.

....

"My concern is not whether you have failed, but whether you are content with your failure."
- Abraham Lincoln

....

Don't be content with failure. Don't be content with letting something go if it's what you really want. After I was let go by one police department half way through the academy, I didn't let that keep me down. I got back up, started working out again, and began testing for more police departments. At the time, it's what I thought I wanted so badly that I would push and push until I achieved it. I had an offer from another department, but came to the realization that law enforcement wasn't exactly what I wanted, and wasn't where I would provide the world the most value in the long run. And I'm ok with that, in fact, I'm ecstatic that I figured it out when I did, rather than investing 25 years of my life to something I wouldn't have been in love with.

You never know where your goals are going to lead you. You may reach them and realize that it wasn't what you were after all along. That's ok. It's all part of the bigger journey and the bigger picture of you improving your life and figuring out how you can provide more value to the world.

Do Good

....

"When I do good, I feel good. When I do bad, I feel bad. That's my religion." Abraham Lincoln

....

You'll gain far more pleasure from doing the good things in life than trying to be mischievous. I had my moments, and many of them were fun at the time, but that was when I was a kid. As I've grown older, I've begun to realize that the pleasure I experienced with my friends pulling pranks or egging someone's house caused them pain or frustration, and that's something I choose not to inflict on people whenever possible.

Never underestimate the power of a good deed. Don't hesitate to help someone that obviously could use a hand. It's a reality that you may not always act in the best interests of other people, we are as humans often self-serving, but you should aim to have the best intentions at all times.

Don't Be Afraid To Give Compliments

Compliment other people. If you like something about them, compliment it. It makes them feel good, you will feel good for passing on those feelings and you build a closer bond with that person. Never aim to do it with an ulterior motive. Done with good intentions, it will reap its own rewards. Everyone loves to receive compliments; it boosts our ego and makes us feel better about ourselves.

Console

Learn how to console people. There will be times in your life when someone needs a shoulder to cry on. It's incredibly powerful to be able to be that person. The type of person who can remain strong despite the rush of emotions.

It's ok to feel those emotions too. I'm not saying you have to be a sturdy rock with no feelings. That's not useful to them or you. What I am saying is that people need a shoulder to lean on in emotional times, and you've got a pretty nice shoulder for that.

Hug A Dog (or let them use you as a pillow)

Take a second and give a dog a hug. They need love and attention just as much as we do.

Appreciate animals. While we may keep them captive as our pets, they have a mind and a soul of their own. Respect them, pay attention to them and play with them. They may be just a small part of our lives, but we're a huge part of their lives, don't take that for granted.

Share With Others

Share with others. Share your ideas. Share your life. Share your experiences. You never know when one of those things could change their life.

Be Completely Exhausted

Know what it's like to be completely exhausted. To have given your all, your everything towards something. And then strive to reach that pinnacle whenever it's appropriate.

Know what it's like to be completely tired, that feeling where you can barely stay awake. And then try to avoid that feeling as often as possible. Get sleep. There's no glory in trying to work through pure mental exhaustion.

Your body and mind need rest to be able to operate at their peak performance. Take pride in the fact that you're well rested and your mind is in a peak state. You'll be able to work circles around those that try to work relentlessly and never stop to rest.

Learn to Breathe

Learn how to really breathe. Assuming you're in a place that's not polluted and filthy, learn to take deep breaths, enjoy the fresh air and beautiful scents. It's easy to forget how many amazing smells we're given to take in. Stop, breathe and take a moment to let it all sink in.

This idea really hit home with me one day when our dog Dallas was walking along the sidewalk back towards the house, she stopped dead in her tracks, turned her head and took a few deep breaths of some flowers. Then she trotted on her way. If a dog can understand the importance of taking a couple seconds to stop and smell the flowers, surely we can do the same.

Do Not Disturb
>Do not disturb a man when he's eating.
>Do not disturb a man when he's sleeping.
>Do not disturb a man when he's thinking.

Follow those three tenants and have others follow them with you. Why? Because these three things are vital to your success. Your nourishment and your sleep feed your mind. And when your mind is in its active state of thinking, you can't afford the interruptions. They take you out of your peak state. Those interruptions will side track you and take your focus off of your work. That focus will ultimately be the key to your success.

Courage
We tend to think of firefighters, police officers and military personnel as courageous. And they are, there's no doubt about that. Their jobs are difficult ones in the best of times. But anyone can be courageous in their life. It doesn't take running into a burning building or facing down an entire army to be courageous. It could be battling your own fears, standing up for what you believe in or even putting yourself outside of your comfort zone so you can grow.

We all possess courage, some varying degrees that they're comfortable expressing, but we all possess it, and we can all grow it. It's like anything in life, the more you practice doing it, the better you'll get at it. So when you find yourself in situations where you need courage, push yourself to muster the guts and do it. It will get easier each time.

Connect With People

Connect with other people. You have an amazing ability to leverage other people's minds to help push your life further ahead. Everyone has knowledge, skills and experience that you simply don't yet possess. And you may never need to possess if you learn how to truly connect with people that can share those things with you. And likewise, you can share your experiences, knowledge and skills with other people to help them move further along their path.

Temptations

Don't resist all temptations in life. Sometimes you must indulge yourself and go for it. Use a reasonable mind and consider your actions, but don't hold yourself back from all the great things in life simply because you once heard you should avoid temptations.

Train your mind to be able to control your temptations in the first place and you will never really face the wrath of a mind that can't control itself in those situations. Far easier said than done, I know, I'm still working on it.

Hurry

There are few times in your life when you truly need to be in a hurry, very few. You'll know when those moments hit. They usually involve some sort of life or death situation, serious medicals or real life emergencies. Society loves to put everyone into a rushed state, speeding up their perception of time and reality.

Slow your life down. Enjoy the moments you're experiencing. Take your time to enjoy a beautiful sunset over the river or mountains. Stop and smell the flowers. Go cloud spotting. Plan a day with nothing to do, except to get to know yourself and where you want to head in life. Trust me, it's worth it to slow your life down while everyone else goes hurrying by, missing the point of life altogether.

Frolic

Frolic in the meadows of life experiences. Try new things. Explore new ideas. Open up your mind all of the amazing opportunities this world is filled with.

....

"What counts in life is not the mere fact that we have lived. It is what difference we have made to the lives of others that will determine the significance of the life we lead."
– Nelson Mandela
....

Stretch Your Mind

Constant growth is the game. The best way to do that is to exercise your mind daily. Put yourself through mental tests, push your imagination to come up with new and exciting ideas and try new things. You'll be amazed at the results you'll be able to achieve.

Doubt

There will be moments in your life when you will doubt yourself. You will doubt your abilities. You will doubt your worthiness. There will be an unlimited number of doubts that will cross your mind.

These are mere thoughts. Thoughts that you, and you alone created in your head. You can, and you must prevail over them if you want to achieve the greatest things in your life. It all comes down to your mindset. Choose to conquer those doubts, and there is little that can stop you from achieving your wildest dreams.

Try New Things

Try new things. You may find a skill set you're amazing at. You may fail completely. But the idea is that you open yourself up to new and creative things that you ordinarily wouldn't consider.

....

"The greatest glory in living lies not in never falling, but in RISING every time you fall."

– Nelson Mandela

....

Part Three: Achievement

Building Personal Empires: Achievement

There will be a lot you want to achieve in your lifetime. The best part about that is that you get to set the course. You, and you alone will define what it means to be successful. And you are the only one who will know if you have actually arrived. The key is to actually set a course with real goals and defined milestones so you know you have arrived.

Sure, there will be a lot of outside influence from society, friends, family and employers, but very little of that matters. If you choose to define your life in a certain way that does no harm to others, but may not fit exactly the same way society as a whole thinks it should, that's ok.

Take your Great Aunt Kim for example. After years of working in the real estate industry and succeeding wildly, things took a major down turn. It took some time, but she was able to shift gears and began living a life more aligned with who she had become. As I write this, she's currently living in Turkey and working as a teacher while exploring the world on her terms. To say I'm jealous would be an understatement.

Jealous not because she's in Turkey (I have little desire to go there), but jealous because she's living a life that inspires her. I'm sure there are ups and downs every day, but that's life.

This part is going to cover a lot of success topics, but the important thing is to note that most of it is how to achieve success, not necessarily what success is. You can define what that means to you, just take the tools in this part and use them to help you achieve your goals.

> ....
> "Success is the sum of small efforts, repeated day-in and day-out."
> – Robert Collier
> ....

Goals - How to Win Every time

I want you to achieve a lot in this life. But I want you to achieve the things that you want, not things that your mother or I are shoving down your throat. I don't care if you don't want to become a Doctor or Lawyer, in fact, those seem like the least obvious career paths you may take at this point.

Regardless, whatever you decide to pursue in this life should be something you're in love with, not what someone else decides you should do. That's not to say you shouldn't listen when we give you advice, often we're just trying to help save you time, grief and hassle by letting you know what we've experienced in our lives.

I really want this letter to be about your goals though. How you can set them and then set yourself up for a win every single time (or at least most of the time.) It's taken me a long time to learn how to set goals, and I'm still trying to figure out how to never fail at them, but I'm hoping this advice can help you get there even faster.

1. **Make Sure It's A Goal You Want To Pursue** - If these goals aren't set by you, you'll have no passion or motivation to see them through. Don't just blindly accept a goal as your own because someone else thinks it should be.

2. **There Needs To Be An Incentive** - Goals are nice. They make you feel good that you're pushing yourself towards something. But why are you trying to achieve it? What's the desired outcome for you? If you can't easily answer that question, perhaps you shouldn't be pursuing that goal.

Let's take weight loss for example. I've battled with this time and time again, but often with little success. There just wasn't enough of a reason to really kick myself into gear to lose the 15 - 20 pounds. That was until I realized how important it was for me to be around to see you grow up. That means more to me than eating that extra bowl of ice cream now.

3. **You Need Accountability** - A goal on paper that you just keep is ok. But it's a hundred times harder to achieve than one you openly share with someone. When someone else knows you're trying to achieve something, they can help keep you on track, provide motivation and guidance, all of which are necessary to get you there. Use someone you know will keep you on track and isn't afraid to confront you.

4. **Motivation** - You'll have all the motivation you need when you first set a goal, but the problem is that the further and further out you get from that initial goal setting stage, the harder it gets to motivate yourself. Find things that keep you inspired and fit with the goals you're trying to achieve. Ex: I want to connect with nature more, so when the weather is nice, I do most of my work outside. It's a simple

way to connect with nature, but it keeps me more motivated and inspired on a daily basis.
5. **Start Small** - Yes, set a big goal for yourself, but break it down into smaller goals that you can easily achieve. When you do this, you create little wins that will develop a successful track record, which motivates you more.

It's impossible to know nothing about space flight and say you want to get to Pluto next month. Instead, you need to start by setting small goals, like "let me see on paper how long it will take to get to Pluto." Then you can take that information and properly plan the rest of your goal.

6. **Set Realistic Timeframes** - It takes time to achieve your goals, and that's ok. Be realistic about how long it will take you to achieve something. You won't be able to lose 40 lbs in a month, so don't make that your goal, you'll be setting yourself up for failure.
7. **Keep These Goals Constantly In Mind** - Print them out, write them up, make notes and put them all over the place. You need to be constantly reminded of your goals and what you're trying to achieve, otherwise it will shift to the back of your mind.
8. **You're Going To Stumble** - Listen, you're going to fail at times while trying to achieve your goals. It's just a part of life and the mission you're on. That's ok. If you forgot to workout one day, it's ok, get back into it the next day. A small set back isn't going to end your goal, just keep on pushing.

9. **Squash Negative Thoughts** - The world is chock full of negativity. Do your best to push it out of your life. Think of the positive, the good things you have in life, how far you've come and everything you're about to achieve. Having a positive mindset makes all the difference.
10. **Get Help** - It's hard to achieve your goals alone. Get some help, whether it's professional or just a good friend who's been through the same struggle. Having someone that can support you as you make your way towards your goal can help immensely, especially when you're hitting those dips.
11. **Reward Yourself Often** - When you hit milestones in your goal, don't be afraid to reward yourself. It will help keep you motivated and pushing towards your next goal so you can get another reward. Make sure those rewards don't set you off track ex: weight loss reward would be video games, not ice cream. Don't go overboard with the rewards, just enough to make you feel good for accomplishing your milestone.
12. **Visualize Your Goals** - Take time daily to visualize yourself having achieved your goal. How good will you feel? Will it be everything you thought it would be? This helps you keep your goal in your mind in a positive manner. You can begin to experience all the positives that are going to come from it, but long before you actually achieve it.
13. **"Never, Never, Never, Never Give Up"** - Winston Churchill - If it really matters to you and where you're going in this life. Don't you dare ever give up. You may fall back a bit, but keep moving

forward. Don't let anyone or anything get in your way. There is always a way to achieve what you're after, so don't stop pushing until you achieve it.

14. Create Back Up Plans - For every goal you have, there will be a process you plan to use to achieve it. For every step, you need to create a backup plan in case it fails for some reason, you'll have an immediate plan of action to keep moving yourself forward.

This isn't by any means a comprehensive plan to make sure you never ever fail, but it should serve as a great guideline to use for every goal you set.

Being In The Zone

....

"You must expect great things of yourself before you can do them."
- Michael Jordan

....

There's a special sweet spot that you can get to when you find the work you love, many people call it being in the zone. It's something you could do all day long every day and not think twice about why you're doing it. In fact, when you're in the zone, you're so laser focused that many things that would normally be a priority for you drift to the back of your mind. When you spend more time doing the things you love, it becomes easy to get into the zone.

Getting into the zone is an incredible experience to have, and one you should aim to have often. To make that happen, you need to figure out what the zone looks like to you, how you got there before and then figure out how to cultivate that in the future. This may sound confusing, rest assured, I'll explain it to you in more detail in the future, but this book contains many of things you'll need to do to get there.

Challenge The Status Quo

Most people are ok with floating through life and doing the minimum to get by. Because of this, they will sit there and blindly follow 'the rules', which aren't really rules. They are the standards that everyone just happens to fall into, societies norms if you will.

I want to tell you, it's ok to challenge those standards. As long as you're within the confines of the law, go for it.

There's no glory in always following the herd. Instead, break free and become the leader.

You'll find an amazing amount of opportunities come your way when you're no longer just a part of the crowd, but instead leading the way others are thinking and acting.

Aside from opportunities that are going to come your way, you'll be more inspired to create the life you want to live. And in fact, it's only possible to create the life you truly want when you're not stuck following the same rules that everyone else blindly does.

....

"Don't be afraid to challenge the status quo, it's the only sure way to know you're doing something extraordinary." - Chris Lockwood

....

Hard Work Is The Only Route To Success

I love shortcuts. They save time, energy, and usually get you results in a fraction of the time. But one thing I've learned over the years is that many of the shortcuts you try to take will only lead to more work down the road.

I always think there has to be a faster or easier way to do something because I'm inherently lazy. Like most people, it's in our DNA to expend the least amount of energy for the greatest gain. But here's the honest truth, it rarely pans out.

I've tried finding book summaries to write reports instead of reading the book (they never came out great) and I've tried to take short cuts to repair things only to have them fall apart on me. The shortcuts may work for a short time, heck, they may even get you a passing grade, but they never work as well as actually doing the hard work. And most of all, you won't learn the lessons when you try to shortcut your way through life.

The biggest successes that I've had in my life can all be traced back to real, honest, hard work. You see, the <u>key to really succeeding is putting in the extra effort when everyone else is trying to find the shortcuts.</u> Look at any of the world's most successful people, like them or hate them, they all worked incredibly hard to get there. They did things that others weren't willing to do, they invested the time and energy to develop their skills and experience.

Along that path, there may be methods that can help you save time like finding a good mentor or taking the right classes. But when it comes to building your future and doing all of the amazing things you want to do in this world, you'll never do it if you're constantly seeking the shortcut in life.

It's incredibly tempting to be lazy and find the shortest route. I'm 100% guilty of it myself. But when I've been in those times, I've probably spent more time and energy trying to find a shortcut than it would have actually taken me to do the work.

Success takes hard work. It takes perseverance to push through the hard times. And it takes passion, you must love what you're doing.

When you combine those three things together, you're far more likely to reach your goals. Take this book for example. When I was growing up, I never thought about writing a book, now I have multiple books being written. And let me tell you, it's A LOT of work to write a book.

Sitting down to write day in and day out isn't always fun, but I push myself to do it because I want to get my message out to you in a way that will last forever and ultimately I love the idea of what I'm putting together here.

So the next time you have something you need to get completed, roll up your sleeves and get to work, you'll be rewarded far better if you just do it versus trying to find every possible short cut you can.

....

"Develop success from failures. Discouragement and failure are two of the surest stepping stones to success."
– Dale Carnegie
....

Life Is Full Of Opportunities

As you go through life, you're going to find it's chock full of opportunities. Some you'll see staring blindly in your face, others you may have to dig a little bit deeper to get to. I've spent most of my days tumbling through life like most people, just taking whatever comes my way and while I seized many opportunities, I didn't go after so many others that I should have.

It's easy to get talked out of following opportunities that present themselves to you. People are always eager to give their input. They'll tell you things like "that's too risky", "that will never work out," or "you shouldn't waste your time on that." And most of the time their advice is well intended, people want to help you out as best they can.

But here's the key. Just because they haven't had success with something before, or they can't see the same opportunity that you do, doesn't mean they're right. Instead, take their input, ask them why so you can get a deeper perspective of what they see and use that as part of your decision making.

I can almost guarantee you that the older you get, the more you and I will run into this problem together. I'm sure there will be times where I shoot you down before you can even fully explain something to me. I give you permission now to find a way to get through to me so we can truly dig into it and see each other's sides.

Back to these opportunities though, I want to talk to you about what they are, when they're going to appear and what they really mean to you so you can make the most use of them when they show up. The biggest problem people face is this shiny object syndrome where they get an idea put in front of them, they think they can use that to solve all of their problems, be them money, relationships, work, etc.

I'm here to level you down to earth. There are no short cuts to reaching success in any part of your life. I'm sorry, but it's true. If you want to have the best of everything, you're going to have to work for it, but that's where seizing opportunities comes to your advantage. When you can find the opportunities, understand them and use them, you can gain an advantage that nobody can take away from you, especially since they'll be off following the next shiny object that crossed their path.

So about these opportunities, some you can create, others will be created for you. It's that simple. It either breaks down to you taking action to achieve something in your life, thus you created the ability for an opportunity to come up, or someone else was working along their path and opened up something that you can use as an opportunity for yourself.

Don't sit back and wait for the latter though. Those are going to be much fewer and further in between than if you decide to take action and create your own. Think about it, you could wait years and years for someone to present a new job opportunity for you, or you could go out and create your own business doing that exact job right? Maybe you have no desire to be an entrepreneur, that's fine, you can use this same principle in any walk of life.

Let's say you want to have a better relationship, instead of sitting back and hoping that they'll begin to do more dishes or laundry because they never do, you need to open up and express that to them. Talk about it and open a dialogue, that's how you create the opportunity for a better relationship. If you sit back and wait for them to realize there's a problem, you're going to be waiting a long time.

This all leads back to the idea that if you're hoping for something to happen, stop just hoping for it, and make it happen. We all have a lot more power and ability than we give ourselves credit for, so now it's time to harness it and make those opportunities come to you.

If you don't take the time to seize these opportunities, someone else will do it instead.

....

"The starting point of all achievement is desire."
– Napolean Hill

....

Life Is Not All About Money

Life is not all about money.... But it sure does help.

For years, I always lived the mentality that "I don't need to be super rich, I just need enough to get by and a little extra to save." It's a great theory right? Not taking more than you need, and still being able to save for retirement.

I'm sorry to say, and this may piss off some people, but I'm not out to appease everyone reading this book, but that mentality is completely wrong. Now that I think about it, it's the most asinine thing I could have said.

Why? It's the totally wrong way to think. When you think small, you receive small. When you think big, you will receive big.

So why do I want to be a multi-millionaire?

I've thought long and hard about this because it took a total reframing of my mind to get here. I can break it down to two major things.

1. I never want to worry about being able to provide for my family.
2. I want to give back so so much to environmental, conservation and public safety causes, but I could never do that properly if I was just making ends meet.

Receiving oodles of money is about far more than just me. I have little to no motivation to go out and buy Lamborghini's, massive mansions and personal jets. That's just not me. But if I could help my family members out, and be able to give back to those things that I love so much in this life, that's what gets me excited.

I don't expect you to agree with everything I say here, I know money is a sensitive issue for people, but I think you can see where I'm coming from. The more money I make, the more money I can use to give back and help other people.

It's for that exact reason that from day 1, any business I start is designed to give back. Because it makes sense for my personal goals and what I'm trying to achieve in this world. Did you know that some of America's wealthiest people are also the biggest supporters of charities? Most people never stop to think about that or really look into it. John D. Rockefeller has his place in history. Many people think of him as a giant tyrant who took control of everything he could and at any cost.

While there may be some validity to that. He was also a major supporter of environmental projects. He helped finance, design and oversee construction of the carriage trails in Acadia National Park in Maine. I would love to be wealthy enough to help support something similar. But even if I never reach that level, I will guarantee you that I will leave a positive impact on this place we call earth.

Maximize Your Time

Life is filled with waiting, and I hate waiting. It's one of my biggest pet peeves. But rather than sit there and grumble about it all the time, I've found ways to get around that. I'm constantly looking for ways to fill my down time, which now mostly consists of me writing or brainstorming new ideas for projects when I'm stuck waiting.

My job as a 911 dispatcher can be painful, long long hours with nothing to do except watch tv or surf the internet. Instead of sitting there bored all the time (there were still a lot of bored moments though), I took the initiative to use the slow periods to get work done. I went to school full time and got my bachelor's degree, attempted several small businesses and even wrote most of this book. It's not always easy to stay on track with my thoughts since I have constant interruptions, but that's just something I have to deal with since I'm lucky enough to even have the time and ability to do these things while being paid.

You should do the same thing with your time. Even if you find yourself doing nothing more than dreaming about all the great things you're going to have in life, and how you'll achieve them. That's far better than most people will ever do when they're stuck waiting somewhere.

Push Yourself As Hard As You Can Towards Your Goals

Nobody ever reached the top and stayed there by taking the easy route. If you ever want to achieve amazing things (and I certainly hope you do), you'll have to work harder and longer than the average American. It's not an option. It's an absolute necessity.

You can easily observe where people are in life based on how much energy and sacrifice they are willing to put into things. Many of the poorest and least successful people in well-established countries are in that position because they lack the same effort as those that chose to become successful.

There's absolutely no one else to blame. It's not the government's fault, it's not my fault, it's not corporate America's fault. If you want something, and you don't yet have it, it's because you haven't put in the effort and energy to achieve it.

I wish I could stand in front of you and tell you that this has always been my golden rule, but I can't. For a long time, I was lazy, did the bare minimum to get by in almost everything I was doing. It wasn't until around the time you were born that I realized I needed to make massive changes in my life.

Those changes took time, and yes they took a lot of energy and sacrifice. But the reality is that because I sacrificed so much earlier on, I'm now able to see the dividends of that investment. It takes time. Heck, I'm still not where I want to be in life, but I'm well on my way.

And I'm doing this all under my own power. I'm not sitting back waiting for someone to drop success in my lap, because I know that will never happen. I AM RESPONSIBLE FOR MY FUTURE. Just as you are responsible for your future.

> "People who succeed have momentum. The more they succeed, the more they want to succeed, and the more they find a way to succeed. Similarly, when someone is failing, the tendency is to get on a downward spiral that can even become a self-fulfilling prophecy."
>
> – Tony Robbins

Take Pride In Your Accomplishments

I'm working hard to raise both you and your brother to be good people. That I will never compromise on. And every time you take a step forward to becoming an awesome person, I'm excited.

We're going to be an extremely hard working family. The kind that never cuts corners to achieve our goals and make our dreams come to reality. And because we're going to work so damn hard to make it in this world, I want you to make sure you take the time to appreciate everything you achieve.

Most people float through life with little direction, working to make ends meet and living a boring life. I want our lives to be filled with excitement, and filled with our true selves. Do what inspires you in life.

I know you're still young now, but when you grow up, you're going to find passions. Those things that you couldn't live without. Follow them. Don't compromise.

It won't always be easy to find the path in the dark, but trust me, it's there. If you stay true to yourself and those things that make you feel alive, you'll find your way.

And when you finally arrive where you're supposed to be, revel in that. Be proud that you followed the path that made your life worth living.

The Most Important Accomplishments
....

"People often say that motivation doesn't last. Well, neither does bathing – that's why we recommend it daily."
– Zig Ziglar
....

The most important accomplishments in your life are going to come purely because of your motivations and ambitions. It's important to remember that along the way. When you achieve a big goal in your life, even if others played a part in making it happen, you were a driving force in that as well. Get excited and be proud of your accomplishments.

It's easy to be humble and not think they're very exciting, but to others, the things you're accomplishing could be nearly super human feats. At 18, I became a certified firefighter, by 23 I was the Captain of a fire house. I don't say that to try and impress you, or get you to exceed my accomplishments, I just want to point out that those are major goals. There are countless people who at 45 or 50 still wouldn't dare to ever think about becoming a volunteer firefighter.

But to me, being a firefighter is just part of who I am, it's engrained in the very core of who I am at this point in my life, so it's easy to overlook those things as a major accomplishment, but they are. I devoted thousands of hours to learning and maintaining these skills.

When you accomplish something big in your life, take the time to acknowledge all the hard work you put In to get there, because there are countless people who wouldn't dare to work as hard as you, and because of that, they'll never achieve a fraction of what you will.

Why Resolutions Fail

....

> "Real difficulties can be overcome; it is only the imaginary ones that are unconquerable."
> – Theodore N. Vail

....

Every year, people choose a couple of resolutions to try and make their life better. And yet very few people ever follow through and see success. Why? It's simple. They lack a formula for achieving their goals. That formula that I use?

1. Pick measurable goals – If you can't measure it, you won't know if you're progressing.
2. Make sure they matter to you – If you don't care about what you're working towards, how on earth could you ever motivate yourself to take the right actions?
3. Have a method of tracking them – Keep track of what you're pursuing.
4. Break each goal down into chunks – Break the big picture into smaller, bite sized chunks that you can tackle one piece at a time.
5. Set deadlines – Set clear deadlines that you must achieve each chunk by.
6. Have a backup plan – Plans often go astray, make sure you have an alternate plan you can divert to if needed.

7. Accountability – Have someone hold you accountable to your goals. You'll feel like there's a lot more on the line when you have to report your progress to someone else. (On that note, make sure that person is reliable and will keep you on track.)

8. Set Reminders – It's easy to get side tracked and forget the big picture. Find a way to consistently remind yourself in new and creative ways.

9. Have rewards – When you achieve each chunk, have a way to reward yourself for that. It gives you something to look forward to and work toward.

Always Seek Feedback

It's not always pretty, and it's not always right, but it can help you grow faster.

Being open to feedback can be difficult. It puts you in a vulnerable position, which we are almost always seeking to avoid. But the reality is that feedback is one of the best things you can do to increase your growth.

Listen when people have input. Gauge it and use it as you see fit, but always be open to listening. If nothing else, it will show them that you respect their opinions and value their friendship or leadership abilities.

....

"When you learn, teach. When you get, give"
– Maya Angelou

....

Develop A Skill

Develop a skill that is useful to the world. That skill should help you provide real, tangible value to others. Don't just learn skills to make money or worse to try and impress others.

There have been plenty of moments in my life where I passed on learning a skill because I knew I wouldn't be able to maximize it enough to provide more value to the world. That's not always an easy decision to make, but it's often the right one if you're going to live a life that's truly yours.

There are two schools of thought on developing skills. The first is that you should lean into and focus on the things you find yourself naturally talented at. The second is to find the areas where you're weak and to grow those. Personally, I would go with the first. Find areas that you can more easily excel at because you'll be able to provide more value to the world sooner and at a higher level.

Going this route doesn't mean you can't continue to grow and level up the areas where you're weak, but they shouldn't be your primary driver. Focus the bulk of your energy on the areas where you can provide the highest value to others and then fill in your time growing and pushing yourself in other ways.

Learn From Experimentation

The absolute best way to truly and deeply learn anything is to learn through experimentation and failure. When you fail at something, that failure becomes a rooted memory. It gives you something to build from, something you can avoid in the future if necessary. Those that learn only from books and other people's successes are depriving themselves of a real education. I believe whole heartedly in learning as much as possible from others and through those books, but after you've done that, you need to go out and try. You need to put your effort in, fail forward fast. A great quote from Thomas Edison sums this all up perfectly: "I have not failed. I've just found 10,000 ways that won't work."

Don't Settle

....

"You've got to find what you love... Your work is going to fill a large part of your life, and the only way to be truly satisfied is to do what you believe is great work. And the only way to do great work is to love what you do. If you haven't found it yet, keep looking. Don't settle. As with all matters of the heart, you'll know when you find it."

– Steve Jobs

....

It Always Seems Impossible

When we set out to achieve something big in our lives, it's difficult to see how we'll get to the end goal. Take it bit by bit and tackle one thing at a time and you'll surely reach your goal. Try too hard to jump to the end without dealing with all of the middle ground and you'll be facing an uphill battle the entire way.

....

"It always seems impossible until it's done."
– Nelson Mandela

....

Everything You Know
"When you grow up you tend to get told that the world is the way it is and your life is just to live your life and try not to bash into the walls too much...that's a very limited life. Life can be much broader once you discover one simple fact--everything around you that you call life was made up by people that were no smarter than you...shake off this erroneous notion that life is there and you're just going to live in it versus make your mark upon it. Once you learn that, you will never be the same again."
- Steve Jobs

Self-Guided Education
Self-guided education will always produce better results than one forced upon you. Guide your own education. You'll invest more time and energy into it. I've gotten way more out of a couple of years of self-directed education based on what I wanted to learn than I did in all of the time I invested in formal schooling.

There are a couple of keys there though. Learn about the things that interest you most in life, make sure they have some long term pay off for you, even if it's just for a cathartic reason. And you MUST be committed to continually pursuing education on your own without anyone there to motivate you

....

"Self-education makes great men." -Bruce Lee

....

Work Harder

I want you to work harder than I did. I want you to put in more effort, more consistently than I ever did so you can achieve things on a level I only dreamed of. Work smarter too. Smarter and harder and you'll become nearly unstoppable in what you're out to achieve.

....

"I'm a great believer in luck, and I find the harder I work, the more I have of it." - Thomas Jefferson

....

Your Idea

"Your idea may shorten the war."

This was a slogan that was used during World War 2 in the U.S. to promote people to come up with ideas and bring them forward. The idea is still relevant and can be used even in your day to day life as you battle your own wars. Take time to think and explore your mind, you never know what ideas you'll come up with.

In 2014 I started working on Idea Factory - it was a personal thing, not some awesome business, but it's important regardless. With Idea Factory, I spend 15 minutes, ideally several times a week to do a pure brainstorm on a single idea with the goal of coming up with 10 new ideas.

Here's the principle behind it. Coming up with one or two ideas for something is easy. 10 gets much more difficult. And having a clear time frame to work under forces your mind to stay active and focused on coming up with ideas. The idea factory has single handedly helped my mind to shift from a problem and single solution mindset to one of problem and numerous solutions.

Why does that matter? Because not everything in life is going to succeed on the first attempt. Often, we're going to find ourselves in need of more than one solution to a problem. So when idea one fails, and it will, I can immediately shift to idea number 2, 6, 8, whatever I need to make it succeed. It makes me faster to react, and that's vital to getting ahead in life. The world responds well to action takers.

....

"Most of the important things in the world have been accomplished by people who have kept on trying when there seemed to be no help at all."
– Dale Carnegie

....

Small Thinking

Small thinking gets you small results. Big thinking gets you big results, so think big if you want to win.

You Are Far More Powerful Than You Know

You are far more powerful than you know. You can accomplish anything with hard work and dedication. Success will never just fall into your lap. You have to work for it, push yourself and devote everything you have to get there, but when you do that, and you push through all the barriers that will be put in your way, you realize just how incredibly powerful you really are.

Greatest Time

You were born into one of the most amazing times. You have more information and resources at your disposal than at any point in history, so make use of them. There are no excuses to not set out and reach your ultimate goals, no excuses except those that you contrive in your mind. And those excuses are just the fiction of your imagination, so wipe the board clean and get started on your life.

Goals

You may not always reach your goals, that's ok. They gave you a target to aim for and a reason to get started. And that's what matters most, getting started on something. Your life is a lot like a ship, you have the ability to aim for a new port if needed, but you first have to steam out of the harbor and into the sea. That means you have to get started, get going on something, if it doesn't turn out to be what you thought you needed or where you wanted to go, you can aim for a new goal, but at least you're under way and have momentum behind you to guide you to a new place.

....

"You've got to get up every morning with determination if you're going to go to bed with satisfaction."
– George Lorimer
....

It's Not the Number Of Hours

It's not the number of hours you put in that determines your success, it's the quality of work done during those hours.

Other People's Opinions

Don't let other people's opinions of you control your destiny.

It's easy to get your mind all tangled up in what other people are thinking of you. And when that happens, you'll often forgo experiences or taking action because you're concerned about what they think. Put that aside. If you feel what you're doing is the right thing for you and will better the world in some way, no matter how small, then do it. Take action and don't worry about what other people are thinking.

I know that's easier said than done right? It will take time and a lot of focused thoughts to work through it, but that's what must be done. You must get over worrying about what others think so you can live the life you're meant to live. Setting out to become an entrepreneur hasn't been easy for me, and it goes entirely against the grain of what everyone around me has always done, but that's ok. It's not their life, and it's not their goals that need to be achieved, they're mine, and that's why I'm working towards them. You do the same for your goals.

All Breakthroughs

....

"All breakthroughs happen one shift at a time... and those slight differences can all be counted." - Jesse Elder

....

Every little thing you do to push yourself ahead in life will play a part in getting you there. They often may seem small and inconsequential, but they're helping you towards your goals little by little. The key though is to make sure that what you do is measurable in some way.

Without being able to measure things, you have no real way of knowing if you're actually moving forward or not. You may be able to count them by numbers or through events in your life, but make sure you have some way of keeping track.

Put Your Message Out There

Put your message out there to the world. Share who you are and what you're trying to achieve. This is something I've struggled with most of my life. I've always been concerned with what other people are thinking and how they're going to react to what I'm putting out into the world.

Well, you know what? Even if there are critics (and there always will be), there are people out there waiting for exactly what you're trying to do. They need the help and guidance you can provide to them. So don't hold back, someone needs exactly what you can provide.

It's Possible

If someone before you has done it, then know it's possible for you to do it too. It will take hard work and dedication, but you can do it.

If no one has done it before you, well, then you get to pave the future for others to come behind you. These moments will take far more work, but there's a way to do nearly anything if you set your mind and ambitions to it.

Take Action

You'll never know everything you think you need to know to get started. Get started anyways. You can learn along the way. You'll reach a critical point where you know plenty to get started, and that's when you need to take action. Don't sit on your knowledge and wait for the 'perfect' moment, because that moment may never come.

Shine

Be damn proud of who you are and what you have to offer the world. It's ok to be the guy that shines and people look up to. It's a far better place to be than the person who's always looking up to others.

When you're in that position of authority, you know and understand that you must continue to push yourself and grow if people are going to continue to look up to you. That's what makes being your father so rewarding, because I know if I'm going to have you look up to me and be the man you want to be, then I have to push myself harder and harder to be better, stronger, smarter and also to share those things with you and the world. There's no sense in gaining all of those things if I'm going to keep them to myself.

Perseverance

The best thing you can do when you don't feeling like working on something is to just get started. Lie to yourself. Tell yourself you'll just work on it for five minutes. Put in a serious effort for five minutes. You'll find that you'll push through and keep going.

Pushing through when you don't feel like you can keep going, or like you want to keep going is tough work. But it's necessary if you're going to reach your bigger goals. Do just a little bit more. Or break it down into pieces. I didn't sit down and write this book for you in a week, no, it took months of consistent effort, writing just a few hundred words each day, but eventually it will be completed, only through my persistent and never ending effort to make it happen.

....

"Problems are in your life so that you can discover potentials that you didn't even know you had."
- Barry Michels

....

Procrastination

Procrastination is something I, like many people have become an expert in. Don't try to go down that path too, it's a terrible habit. Instead of getting to work and clearing things from your mind, you end up sitting on them, dwelling, contemplating and then working twice as hard to get them done when they need to be completed. Instead, get started immediately. Give yourself a false deadline if you must, but get started immediately. You'll free your mind and clear yourself to get so much more accomplished in life.

....

"Give me six hours to chop down a tree and I will spend the first four sharpening the axe."
–Abraham Lincoln

....

Get Out Of your Own Way

The biggest reason people fail in life is simply because of themselves. They allow negative thoughts to creep in and take over their minds. Focus on the positive instead. Know that you can achieve anything you want in life. We all have faults, and things we need to work through, there's no escaping that. But any time you find yourself doubting your abilities or skills, shift your mindset, focus on the fact that you have already accomplished so many things in your life that you previously couldn't do, this is just one more on that list.

Negotiate

Learn to negotiate. Terms that are given to you aren't always as they need to be. Being able to negotiate will give you a distinct advantage when you get older.

Nothing Truly Stops You

"Nothing truly stops you. Nothing truly holds you back. For your own will is always within your control... Your will needn't be affected by an incident unless you let it. Remember this with everything that happens to you."
– Epictetus

Go The Extra Mile

"Go the extra mile, it's never crowded." – Unknown

Interruptions

Avoid interruptions at all costs when you're working on something. Every interruption distracts you, draws you away from your objective and makes it harder to regain focus. They cost you time, and that's the one resource we all have an incredibly finite amount of.

I wrote a huge portion of this book, went to college online, and worked on my side businesses while at the dispatch center. I'm grateful for that opportunity, but I know I could have been three times more efficient if I had been able to do all of those things during time where I wasn't constantly interrupted by 911 calls, radio transmissions, etc. Every time I got back into what I was working on, I'd get interrupted again, and even if my partner took care of it, it still got my mind off track.

I've come to love the ability to focus on my projects uninterrupted. I usually put nice big headphones on, throw on some classical music and tune out the world. It's the only way I've found to truly stay on track and working towards my goals, avoiding the rest of the world and focusing on what I needed to get accomplished.

Society is overly connected in ways that breed interruptions from social media to email and the occasional phone call. You have choices though, choices that can change your life. You can choose when and how you'll interact with people. You can create a life that's filled with awesome people but only when it's appropriate. You can establish your life so you're not filled with interruptions. That choice is yours.

Tantrums

Tantrums get you nowhere. I'm writing this section as you're throwing a tantrum about taking a nap. Earlier I had to battle you to get you to go potty. You're 2. I understand it, and I'll deal with it as they come. But even as you get older, and to the adults that may be reading this, understand that tantrums don't work.

If you're not getting your way with something, it doesn't help to fight about it. Instead, invest your energy into finding a solution that will work better for everyone involved. It's far more productive and will push you to think about better solutions.

Don't Wait For The Perfect Time

You can never count on the perfect time for something. It could happen in the blink of an eye, or never at all. It just can't be predicted. That means you need to take action immediately and consistently.

Waiting for the perfect time that may never arrive could set you so far behind where you should be. I've waited for perfect moments in my life, and waited, and waited, yet they never seemed to show up. If you have an idea, a goal, a passion you want to pursue, then seize the day and make it happen, don't wait for perfect, because it may never arrive.

If It Were Easy Everyone Would Do It

If it were easy everyone would do it. Push yourself to do those things in life that don't come easy, that require sacrifice, that require perseverance.

The surest route to success is taking the road less traveled, and that road is filled with difficult obstacles. Face them down, conquer them and push yourself harder than you can imagine.

Then, and only then is success a sure thing because nobody else was willing to put in the time, the energy and the effort to make it happen.

Granted

People who don't do the work will take for granted how much effort you put into becoming successful. Don't ever diminish the effort you put into getting to where you are. Let people know you worked hard, sacrificed when necessary and persevered through the hard times to get where you are. The problem with the perception of successful people is that everyone thinks it was easy for them, or they had one great idea and hit the jackpot. It's not true. The vast majority of these people worked harder and longer than anyone else to see their goals come to fruition. You should do the same.

Make Daily Investments
Make Daily Investments in:

- Your Mind
- Your Body
- Your Soul
- Your Friends
- Your Family
- Your Work/ Passion

What does an investment look like? It looks like whatever you need it to be. For your mind it could be reading or writing. Your body investment could focus on nutrition or exercise. And it goes on and on. The idea though is that you figure out what investments you can make, no matter how small or big and commit to them each and every day. This is the surest way to bring abundance to your life.

....

"When you want to succeed as much as you want to breathe, then you'll be successful." - Unknown

....

Seek Out Mentors

Seek out mentors in your life. People that have achieved what you're trying to get to. Whether they're actual hands on mentors or virtual, seek them out, pay attention to what they have to say and follow their guidance. You'll save yourself a lot of time, angst and frustration trying to learn it all on your own.

Owl Spotting - July 11th 2014

We were outside today playing in the front yard when we heard the distinct sound of an owl hooting and talking with another owl far off in the distance. We could hear her hooting, but it's incredibly difficult to see through the clutter of the leaves in the trees to find her. The same goes for your life. The more you have going on, the more clutter your life has, the more difficult it is to see through it to your end goals. The way around this isn't to wait until fall or winter, because even though the leaves will be gone, so will your target. Focus instead on limiting your input, limit the amount or density of the clutter in your life and finding your target will be a lot easier.

July 15th, 2014

Ordinarily I wouldn't come back and write about the same topic again, but I felt this one was incredibly important. Tonight, as you and I were on our way out to replace the hummingbird feeder with new food, we walked onto the deck. You stopped, said to me (as calm as could be), "Dad, Owl." I turned towards the other side of the deck and sure enough there was a big, beautiful owl sitting on the railing. I put the hummingbird feeder down on a chair and moved back towards the door.

It was startling to see the owl there, I've never been so close to one. And yet a sense of calm came over me. We stared at it for a while, taking in what we thought was going to be just a momentary glimpse. But then a funny thing happened, it didn't move. It stayed there, and stared back at us. So I grabbed my camera to get a few pictures. And the owl sat there, and sat there some more.

It was incredibly powerful, yet humbling to be able to sit there for 30 minutes and stare into the eyes of a wild bird. Eventually, I was able to get within four feet or so of the bird, and never once did it get startled or frightened. I couldn't have asked for a more powerful moment with you. To be able to sit there with you on my lap, staring deep into the owls eyes.

Originally you went back inside to sit just inside the sliding door with Dallas because you were scared. I was able to coax you back out a few times. You of course had questions about it. Whether it was a boy or a girl (I have no idea), what it eats and where it lived. Which of course lead to you inquiring if it had a picnic table in the tree to eat off of. Yes, yes it does.

Nature and the universe send you signs all the time. Pay attention to them. It can often be difficult to decipher exactly what they mean, but pay attention and use those signs to improve your life. If that wasn't a sign from the universe and nature, I couldn't tell you what is.

Breakthroughs

Breakthroughs are those magical moments in your life when you've been striving so incredibly hard towards something and you finally make it. You achieve everything you've been dreaming of. Everything you've been working towards. The only sure way to hit that breakthrough point is to push yourself consistently beyond your comfort zones.

The Success Route

Everybody is constantly on the search for the short cut to success. Let me break this all down for you. There is no true short cut. The only way to cut the process down is to take consistent and intentional actions towards your objective. The people who try to find the easy route never get further ahead, they get stuck at the visitor center while the few who are devoted to learning and taking action steadily move their way up the side of the mountain.

....

"The only sure way to success is to set goals and achieve them, constantly."
- Chris Lockwood

....

Greatness

"Greatness is not this wonderful, esoteric, elusive, god-like feature that only the special among us will ever taste - you know it's something that truly exists in all of us.

It's very simple, this is what I believe and I'm willing to die for it. Period. It's that simple. And that's all I need to know, so from there you do what you need to do. I think what happens is we make this situation more complex than it has to be (because we're looking for complexity)."
- Will Smith

Conquering Your Fears

I have a challenge for you: Those things you fear most in your life. I want you to conquer them. Embrace them rather than retreating from them.

Take time to learn about your fears and you'll take away all the power they hold over you. Let's say you hate spiders (basic, I know but a lot of people hate them), learn about their habits, the way they live and the benefits they actually provide to you. I don't suspect you'll fall in love with them immediately, but you'll open yourself up to curiosity.

And curiosity is where we learn best and embrace our new knowledge. In time, you'll find yourself more open to those things you feared and far less afraid. Use this technique for any fear you have. I guarantee you'll make more progress than the retreating you've probably been doing.

Real growth in life comes when we tackle our weaknesses and move beyond them.

Consumption

Consumption of knowledge doesn't make a man great, but rather the power he yields through implementation of that knowledge.

Part Four: Passion

Those Things That Light You Up

Following your passion as a way to create a life is an awe inspiring idea. So many people want to desperately do that, yet they never seem to find a way to make it happen. I've struggled with this time and time again, especially as my passions shift and change.

For a long time I was happy working as a 911 dispatcher. It was fulfilling and most of all, exciting. But over time, my energy drained, the hours began to suck and I lost the drive for it. So I began seeking out alternatives to create a life I was passionate about living and excited to work on every single day. It wasn't an easy thing to work towards, and that's why I wanted to provide you with a small insight into how you can make that process happen easier and faster so you don't have to struggle with it like I have.

Dig around in any number of places and you'll find millions of articles, books, videos, etc about how to find your passion. The surest thing I know is that it's likely to be staring right at you day after day, but you may be blinded to its reality. Uncovering what really inspires you and using that to create your ultimate life isn't an easy task. It will take patience, persistence and faith that it will come to you.

Embrace the journey to get where you're going for it is the journey, not the destiny that makes the man.

Your Passion Becomes Your Work

Too many people get it wrong in life. They work their butts off at a job that they hate, or can barely stand because they think that's what they're supposed to do. Just suck it up, stick it out and you'll earn a good retirement. They get stuck in a cycle where their work becomes their passion.

That's wrong. Your work should never become so much of your life that it's forcibly turned into your passion. Instead, find your passion and turn that into your work. Find that thing you love doing and that you would likely do the rest of your life for free. Find a way to make that profitable and helpful to other people and you'll live a life full of passion, not to mention work will be exciting for you.

....

"A life worth living is not worth sacrificing for things you're not passionate about."

-Chris Lockwood

....

Make Sure You Do What You Love In Life

Don't ever, ever, let anyone talk you out of doing what you love in life. Well, that is as long as it's legal, safe, and doesn't hurt anyone else (Fatherly figuring emerging for that part).

Would you like to know the real reason I got into dispatching?

To be entirely honest, it started out looking like a fantastic way to make more money. When I heard about the job, I was working part time at a golf course in town, that was a good gig, driving around golf carts and having fun the whole time. But the dispatch job was a great way to make more money while I was going to school, in fact, I nearly doubled my hourly wage and hours per week instantly. I would have been dumb not to take the job.

And I loved it for a long time. When I started, I wondered why they paid anyone to do that job, because I would have gladly done it for free. It was exciting, thrilling to be in the heart of everything, literally making decisions that meant life and death for people.

I was able to pay for school almost entirely up front, work full time and go to school full time. It really was a great way to get started in life. But I missed out on a lot of what 'college life' should be like. If I could go back, I would call a redo and go to a four year school instead, partied my brains out and taken on a mountain of debt. Not because that was the responsible thing to do, but it would have given me the chance to grow up a little slower.

But we're digressing a bit here. What I really wanted to get at was the fact that the point I'm at in my life now, I'm sick of this job and the lifestyle. Sure, it's provided me a great background, solid finances and a ton of great moments, but it's starting to be soul-sucking.

What do I mean by that? Well, it's become a job, not so much that I hate going to, but I just don't have the same passion for it anymore that I once did. There are a lot of things about it that I don't enjoy anymore. What really drags at me is missing your childhood, seeing you grow up to be an amazing boy, leaving holiday parties to go to work, being ordered in for 4 am. It's not fun.

And your work should be something you love to do every single day. I don't want you to ever end up in a job that puts you in the position I'm in now. And that's why I'm working so hard to get out of it. I want to show you that you can create any job you want in the world if that's what you want.

Every day of your life should be inspiring to yourself and to others, and that's what you need to strive for, not just dollar signs, and not just for steady work. Pump some value into this world, and always, always give more than you take. The world will pay you back in dividends if you follow that simple advice.

....
"People rarely succeed unless they have fun in what they are doing."
–Dale Carnegie
....

Finding Your Passion

Finding your passion may seem like the hardest thing you've ever done. I struggled for years to really figure out what drove me, what inspired me and what made me want to get up every day. I thought it was something that had to be contrived, manmade.

The reality was that nature was what inspired me and made me excited to live. I love finding beautiful places, watching the hawks fly over our house, witnessing nature conquer everything in its path, like a massive tree growing on top of a boulder. You would never think it could be done, but it happens.

It seems like a terrible cliché, but everything I was looking for was right under my nose the entire time. Now maybe you'll have something entirely different that you could look at, read about and admire all day, and that's cool. But I bet when you begin looking, you'll find exactly what you were after was right there all along, you just looked past it.

....

"Take up one idea. Make that one idea your life -- think of it, dream of it, live on that idea. Let the brain, muscles, nerves, every part of your body, be full of that idea, and just leave every other idea alone. This is the way to success."
-Swami Vivekananda

....

Turning Your Passion Into A Career

Turning that passion into a career is an entirely different problem though. Even though I had figured out I loved nature and being outdoors, I was after a lifestyle that wouldn't exactly be conducive to most outdoor jobs. I wanted the freedom to work from anywhere in the world at any time of day so I could take the time I wanted to be with my family, a necessity after giving up so much of it to the public safety lifestyle.

It took me a long time to figure out that all of the marketing skills I was learning could be combined with nature to help other companies that are out there making products and taking people on epic journeys to get better at marketing their services. Looking back it seems like a pretty simple combination, but I let people and thoughts get in the way of what I really should have been striving for. Will it be my forever thing? Who really knows. The greatest thing about growing up now is that we don't really have to have a forever lifestyle. Pensions have disappeared and company loyalty is a thing of the past, you can blaze your own trail, find or create the work that you love to do and you'll be rewarded in your own ways.

Helping Others Through Your Passion

One of the greatest rewards you can receive in life is helping other people. I've always been driven to that in life, which is a big reason I've enjoyed being a firefighter, it constantly puts you in a place where you can help people. Everyone is striving towards their own goals in life, if you can help them get there faster or easier, then you should certainly do so.

The awesomeness of finding your passion is that you can begin to use it to shape other people's lives. You can help them towards their goals and inspire them to achieve amazing things. People want to follow those that are incredibly passionate and enthusiastic about what they're doing. So when you find and harness your passion, use it to help others.

....
A Good Man
A good man fights for himself & his
A great man fights for everyone else.
-Philip DeFranco
....

Do What You Love

Find those things in life that you love to do, that you would do all the time for free and follow that path. I've been pushed in so many directions over the course of my life because I was told I needed to grow up or move on from something. That's nonsense. If there's something you enjoy in your life and it does no harm to anyone else, then by all means do that until you're sick of it. Then and only then you can consider those other things people were telling you to do.

....

"Our greatest fear should not be of failure but of succeeding at things in life that don't really matter."
–Francis Chan

....

....
The Work
"The work you do while you procrastinate is probably the work you should be doing for the rest of your life." – Jessica Hische

....

Follow The Truth

I've experienced few things in my life that felt as right as being outdoors to me. It was a draw and a connection that I couldn't match in many places. After years of acknowledging it, but putting it off or dismissing it at as nothing more than a basic connection, I've come to realize my connection to the outdoors.

It's an incredible feeling when you can finally realize even a tiny sliver of what your greater mission is here. I'm not entirely sure where nature will lead me in the future, but you'll never know entirely where your end goal is. You just have to follow those things that feel right and true to yourself, those things that you just can't seem to shake.

> "There is no chance, no destiny, no fate, that can hinder or control the firm resolve of a determined soul."
> –Ella Wheeler Wilcox

Never Lose That Youthful Spirit

Never lose that youthful spirit. Make sure you have fun, explore the world and laugh often. I was out filming videos of nature for a personal project I was working on the other day. I was at a spot I'd been to many times where two streams merge together into a larger brook, a fantastic swimming hole and camp site.

I set up the camera and started filming when I looked down stream just a bit and saw what looked like a waterfall. I was so damn excited, I ran off down the trail to check it out. It was like that feeling of unwrapping the best gift on Christmas morning.

Never lose that feeling of being able to explore the world and discover new things, you never know when something amazing has been sitting right under your feet the entire time.

Write

Write down your ideas, you never know when one of them will create that spark you desperately need in your life to seek out your passion. This book is just one of the many ways that I'm getting my ideas out of my head and into the real world. Hopefully something in here sparks your creativity or motivates you enough to change your life, if not, well that's ok, just get your own ideas out and write them down so you can look over them in the future.

Finding Your Value Add

One of the hardest things I've struggled with in life was finding where I can provide real added value. I know I've been able to accomplish a lot in public safety as a firefighter and a 911 dispatcher, and I'm sure I've helped change lives because of that work, but I've always wanted something deeper than that. Those jobs are really fixing people's problems, and that's great work, it's absolutely necessary. But finding that thing that I could wake up every morning and be ecstatic to get started at has been my driver for a long time.

It's taken me quite a long time to figure out where I wanted to take my life, and I'm sure that mission will change over time, but I want to help you get on that same path faster and easier. That is what this book is all about, providing you a leg up in life. Most people try to just pass on money to help their kids get started, I think wisdom is far more valuable an asset, and one that most people fail to pass on.

So here's how to find your value add to the world:

1. Follow things that interest you
2. Learn all you can from those
3. Figure out how you can use that to provide value to the world
    - Can you help other people accomplish their goals?
    - Can you get people results faster than they could alone?

✦ Are you providing an experience or knowledge that they can't easily get themselves?
4. Can you make money from that passion?
✦ Would people be willing to pay you for what you're doing?
5. Get started
✦ Take small steps, trial and error to see what works
✦ Grow your passion into something bigger as time goes on

Figuring out what you want to do in life, especially if it's tied to something you enjoy doing can be complicated. It's easy to get discouraged and give up. But I won't let you do that. You can never, ever give up on your dreams and achieving the things you want in life.

To give up is to surrender yourself to being a part of other people's dreams. While it's important to help other people progress and get better in their lives, you also need to achieve your own big wins, which won't happen when you get stuck working towards other people's goals forever.

Don't Lose Sight

It's easy to get distracted with new and enticing things. Don't lose sight of the bigger picture. The best things you're going to achieve in this lifetime won't come instantly. They're going to require serious, continued and hard effort. That's what makes them so worth achieving. Do whatever you must to keep those end goals in sight as you continue to pursue them.

"We had come so far from where we started, and weren't nearly approaching where we had to be, but we were on the road to becoming better." - Maya Angelou

Impact

We all strive to leave an impact on the world. When we're long gone from this planet, it's nice to think that we've done some good and left the world a better place than when we entered it. Following your passion and creating a following of people is a great way to accomplish that.

Creating A Vision

A vision of the future is about something so much bigger than you and your life. It's about inspiring and helping others. Your vision should be clearly defined so people know and understand what they're getting behind.

I've gone through many visions in my life. I started with public safety, becoming a firefighter, then trying for law enforcement. It was a vision I thought was right for me at the time. Over time though, things changed and so did my vision for the right life for me.

Expect that your vision of your life will change through the years. There's nothing wrong with that. In fact, it's a great sign that you're creating progress and change in your life.

Live Your Dreams
There's no better time to live your dreams than the present time. Know what you're after and then go out and get it. Don't let your dreams become distant thoughts and 'one day's'. You may need to sacrifice some things to make them happen, but if they're really worth having, those sacrifices will make all the difference in the world to you in the long run.

....
True Peace Of Mind
"As long as you continue to IGNORE your passion...True peace of mind will elude you."
– Jesse Elder
....

Part Five: Happiness

Your Happy Place

You deserve to be happy. Life can be a struggle at times, but it's also meant to be enjoyed. It should be fairly obvious that the section on happiness is going to show you ways to make that happen for you, but it's about more than that. To be fully happy takes work. You have to pay attention to your mindset and where you're taking your life.

Happiness is a state of mind more than anything else. With the proper work and guidance, you can train yourself to be happy under nearly any circumstances. But I want more than that for you. I want you to be happy because you fulfilled your wildest dreams and set yourself up for big wins.

Dare to dream big, dare to take action on those dreams and dare to live the ultimate life you want. It will take time, there will be many lessons to learn along the way and many setbacks, but ultimately you and your mindset will determine how far you succeed.

The best of your happiness will always begin with the little things in life. Because it's in those small moments that we are able to define our bigger and far grander purposes in life. There's a lot to be said, but I'll just let the wisdom in here do the work for me...

Follow Your Dreams

If there is ever one thing I could tell you is that you need to follow your dreams. There are of course provisions to that statement, in that it should never hurt someone else mentally, physically or financially. But you need to do the things you love most in life, and if possible, use those things to help improve the lives of others.

I've done well for myself so far. I've accomplished many things in ten years that people would work a lifetime for. I've been a volunteer fire fighter, fire instructor, fire captain, 911 dispatcher, hockey coach, opened a business and got my bachelor's degree among so many other things.

While they haven't all been lifelong dreams of mine, at one point each of these achievements were something I wanted to achieve. So I pushed myself to achieve them. I sacrificed a lot to achieve these things, but that's what makes achieving your goals so great. You see the reward for the time and effort you gave up. You know that every sacrifice you made along the way has paid off and you've finally succeed at achieving your goals.

When you get there, relish that moment for a time, but then the next big part kicks in. You'll have to come up with your next big dream, and then sacrifice some more to achieve that one.

Be Amazed By The Little Things In Life

It took me almost my entire life to realize just how important all of the little things in life are. Today was a great morning. When I woke up, I came downstairs to take the dogs out, I stepped outside and realized there were 5 deer in the woods behind our house. They didn't jump or run. Just gave a simple glance and stared back at me for a moment before they went on their way eating leaves.

At the same moment, a chipmunk scurried across the snow and into the bushes. It's the beginning of March, but it's still quite cold. It was just comforting to see some life coming back to the woods.

Later on, as I was walking out the door, you yelled to me "Dad, I have a hug for you." I stopped in my tracks, turned around with a huge smile on my face and walked the few steps back to you. I knelt down and got the biggest hug from you. Talk about starting a day off right.

Ever since I started writing my gratitude down, I seek out these moments. I'm sure they happened quite often before I really started looking for them, but it's amazing how much more I notice them since I shifted my mindset.

Cherish The Little Moments In Your Life

I was having a frustrating evening, mostly self-induced due to stress of my job and trying to get my own business started coupled with cleaning up the house and everything else life brought my way. It was one of those nights where I just wanted to check out, sit down on the couch and watch tv and ignore everything else that was going on. Your mom was giving you and Matt a bubble bath.

As I was cleaning up things around the living room, I heard the best little laughs I've ever heard coming from the two of you. It stopped me dead in my tracks, and my frustrations immediately went away. I ventured into the bathroom to find you using a bath toy, filling it with air and spitting it out into the water, Matt couldn't possibly think anything else was funnier at the time.

    I love these moments, and it's so incredibly easy to miss them as you go throughout your daily life. Most people never stop to look at or truly appreciate the smallest moments in their lives, but I know you'll be different. You'll grow up understanding how important every little thing in life is to the bigger picture. When you fail to stop and look around, you miss out what it really means to be alive.

    I credit being mindful of gratitude on a daily basis for my increased appreciation of moments like these. You see, when you start to think back about what made your day so great, it builds up a powerful muscle in your brain that over time helps you to instantly recognize those moments when they're actually occurring. That power is so freaking amazing, it wakes you up and helps you really appreciate everything you have in life in a way that most people will never understand.

    So take time, be conscious of the little things that you experience, they'll help you live a much more abundant life, that I can guarantee you.

Go On An Adventure

    Get out of your daily life, frequently. The only place you'll learn and grow is if you step outside of your comfort zone, so I want to encourage you to travel, go out and see what the world has to offer.

    Your mother and I are both very much home bodies, so it makes it easy to stay in one spot, but in reality, I get bored here. Not because there isn't anything to do, but because I want to seek out things that inspire me and move me to challenge myself.

    Some of the best memories I have so far in this life have been from my adventures with crazy people like Rich and Troy. Rich nearly got me killed on a kayaking adventure in Quebec, but it was one of the best trips I've ever taken. They have gotten me into more awkward moments and oh crap situations than I could probably recount, and because of that, I have grown as a person.

    There were plenty of times I would have preferred not to have those experiences with them, some may have involved the police, others a fear of being attacked, but nonetheless, they have still helped me grow and learn. Now here's the fatherly advice, don't get involved with the police or vicious mobs of people, it's not the kind of adventure I want you to have. Instead, get out and explore the world, go visit the National Park you've always wanted to see, or check out a city.

    Do it alone, or bring a group of friends to share in the experience. You'll learn a lot about other people and you'll probably learn a lot about yourself in the moment too.

....

> "Living an inspired life should be at the heart of your goals."
> -Chris Lockwood

....

Happiness Is A Mindset

    Everyone wants to be happy, that's what we're all striving for in our daily endeavors. It's part of what makes our lives so exciting and worth striving towards. Inevitably we all reach a point where what we thought we were after isn't cutting it anymore, it's either not exactly what we really wanted or our ideals have changed as we worked towards that goal. All too often though, I see people trying to fill their lives with material items. The latest clothes, watches, cars, televisions, you name it and people are buying it.

While some of these things are necessities, often they're buying things far beyond the basics to try and fill a void. They get that excitement of getting something new, it's an invigorating moment. But it quickly fades and they no longer get the same happiness out of the object as they did when they bought it. So what do they do? They go out and buy something else to try and fill another void and the cycle continues on and on. They wonder why they're broke and have a house filled with stuff they don't use anymore...... gee, I wonder why.

So what do you do instead of going out and looking for retail therapy to create your happiness? You go out and live your life. Get involved in things, get new experiences, work on personal development, learn something new, spend time by yourself and figure out life, hang out with friends, try something new. Just get out there and LIVE.

It's easy to sit in a room and sulk, draw up negative thoughts and to flood your mind with the bad stuff. Instead, make an effort to think about the positive and create the life you want to live by being happy. It's not the material things in life that will make your life great, it's the moments you enjoyed with your friends and family.

Spend Time With Good People

I'll be completely honest with you. I suck at this. I have a hard time keeping in touch with people, especially right now while I'm working on this book because I'm spending countless hours trying to start my own businesses and getting out of my current job as a 911 dispatcher.

I know, that's not a good excuse right? And I know it's not, in fact it's just about the crappiest excuse I could come up with, because now more than ever, I need to be surrounded by good people and having a good time.

I'm not going to sit here and tell you what makes a person good versus not so good, you're smart, even though you're only 2 right now. It's not difficult to know when you're around people that are going to help you move forward in life and not hold you back.

On that note, you need to constantly surround yourself with people that are smarter than you, going to teach you, motivate you and help you achieve everything you're after.

I love the quote "If you're the smartest person in the room, you're in the wrong room." Think about that for a moment. Sure, it feels great to be the smartest person in your class, your work, at your hobby, etc, but it serves you no value. If you're the smartest person, who are you going to learn from and what's going to push you to achieve the next level. Remember there is always another level.

Instead, perhaps you need to walk out of that room and across the hall where you're not the smartest person. Only then will you have people around you that will help you level up.

You can stay in the first room for as long as you like, but remember, you're going to be stagnant and you'll never reach the highest goals you set for yourself.

Don't take this the wrong way, you don't have to kick people out of your life entirely if they aren't smarter than you, but you do need to limit the amount of time you spend with them.

So how do you find the good people you want to spend time with?

There are a few ways available right now, and I'm sure by the time you actually read and understand what I'm writing there will be quite a few more, but we'll get into what I've found that works.

- Volunteer organizations - I've been a volunteer fire fighter since 2002, I surrounded myself with people that thought the same, enjoyed the same things and understood everything I was going through.
- Online - Social media, forums, masterminds, there are literally dozens of ways to meet new people online.
- Friends/Networking - Don't be blunt and tell them you're trying to move beyond them, but if you know they have a connection that would be a good fit for you to know, you can ask for an introduction.
- Classes - Either through formal education or other interests you have, go take a class and when you're there, introduce yourself to other people.

I need to spend more time connecting with friends and actually hanging out with them. Unfortunately having kids often puts a damper on this, not because it has to, but because we create invisible boundaries. We say things like "Well it's going to get too late for the kids" or "It'll be too much work with all the kids around." Those are crappy excuses.

I guess the trouble now is finding those people that are going to fit in with my entrepreneurial mindset and will help push me to the next level. I love learning and growing, and those are the kinds of people I want to spend time with, the ones that are going to challenge me.

What Makes You Tick?

There's a great mystery about our lives. Each of us is inspired, motivated and drawn to entirely different and unique things. What excites one person may be a total detractor for someone else. And yet, deep down, we're all striving for the same things at our core. The ability to be inspired, feel better, be happier and to live the life we always dreamed of.

Figuring out what makes you function at your core is the key to making all of those dreams a reality. Because it's through that core motivation that you find the ability to provide value to the people around you. And through that value that you can realize your own dreams.

Pay attention to the signs. Stop and take in those little moments where you're incredibly happy for an unknown reason. Watch for signs that you're devoutly interested in something. And when you figure these things out, your next task is to find a way to create a life around that.

Laugh

>Laugh at yourself.
>Watch comedies.
>Create funny times with your friends and family.
>It's cathartic

Develop a strong sense of humor. You'll be happier and people love to be around those that can make people laugh, or love to laugh.

Live Somewhere With Seasons

Live somewhere with well-defined seasons. It will give you a greater appreciation of the cycle of life.

Just Be

Spend time just there, be present in the actual moment of what's going on around you. There's no greater feeling than actually being present in life, not dwelling on the past, not planning the future, just being here and now.

Kids are the ultimate super heroes when it comes to being present. If you're grown up and reading this, take some time and get back to your roots as a kid, be present and enjoy the moment. Everything else in the world will be ok for a bit while you enjoy your life. Trust me.

Positive Thinking

I have a confession... I have lived a life surrounded by negativity and it was all intentional. Although I designed my life this way, I never really understood the power of positive and negative thinking. Public safety isn't an easy lifestyle to live by, we're constantly bombarded by death, destruction and mayhem, called at odd hours of the day and during the worst weather. There's no avoiding that since it's what our jobs revolve around. In fact, most people in public safety thrive off of it. They get an adrenaline rush when they're sent to crazy calls.

But no matter how great the man or woman, it will wear on them. Years of bearing witness to some of the worst tragedies man will ever face on this planet will beat you down. Don't get me wrong, it's an incredibly rewarding career or way to volunteer your time, but you have to take some steps to protect yourself.

If you choose to go down this path, make sure you maintain your friendships and interests outside of the lifestyle. It's easy to drift away from everyone outside of it, especially when everyone else at the firehouse or police department 'gets it'. But that's a b.s. excuse for not making the time and maintaining the friendships that got you to where you are today. I didn't heed this advice well, because I had no one to give it to me. The same really goes for anything you get yourself into. You need an escape.

The important part was not letting the negativity of everything we saw and did into my personal life. That's far easier said than done. Everyone loves to ask about what the latest stories are, or what happened in their neighborhood. I have some amazing stories, and stories are fun to tell as much as they are to listen to, but these stories often don't end well. Letting it all go would be nice, and I do a good job of that most of the time, but there are always things that will stick with you for the rest of your life.

I don't mean for this to sound like a rant, but I've lived a large portion of my life surrounded by negativity and tragedy. It wears on you. So I want you to be able to avoid that, focus on the positive side of life. It's harder to do because most people seem afraid to talk about all the awesome things in life for fear that people will think differently about them. Don't let that get to you. Live the life you were meant to live.

I'd rather be surrounded by a group of people that were happy, excited about life, positive and ready to push themselves to achieve better things than what most people are like. Most people sit there in life waiting idly by, hoping that great things will come their way. And then they complain and blame everyone else when 'bad' things happen to them. Think positive and you'll get positive results.

Focus on the positive. It makes you happier, more optimistic and more alert to opportunities. There's plenty of negative things in this world, but there's no reason they need to be on your mind all the time. Let someone else worry about them.

Recharge Your Mind

It's easy to get worn down day after day when you're pushing yourself towards your life's goals and trying to live a great life. It's important to take time for yourself, to reset your mind and relax it. Like any muscle in your body, if you're constantly working it and don't give it time to rest, it will begin to break down until you're forced to rest it.

Take the time to escape technology and constant inputs. Just be in the moments of your life. Try meditation. Experiment with alone time in the woods. Find a way to release all of the thoughts and emotions that build up in your mind over time, it'll lower your stress levels and you'll be able to get back into pushing towards your goals easier.

Simple Life

Live a simple life. You don't need a ton of possessions to make you happier or more successful. The American lifestyle is all about wants, when in reality, we need very little. Instead, fill your life with experiences, people and great moments. That's where you'll make your best investments.

Live In The Moment

Live in the moment as often as you can, you'll experience a greater sense of living than most people ever will.

What exactly is living in the moment? It's taking in exactly what's happening around you, the people, the sounds, the experience, life. The idea is to be fully present, not thinking about what's happening tomorrow or next week or next month. There's plenty of other time in your life to think about those things, but when you're in the heart of living your life, experience it for everything it's worth.

Happy Life

....

"If you want to live a happy life, tie it to a goal, not to people or objects."
 –Albert Einstein

....

Family Above All Else

I have always put my family first. It's been the most important thing to me. When I started working, I would always try to take the holiday's off even though I was scheduled to work in the dispatch center. It became a million times more important to me when you came along. There was no way I wanted to miss out on Christmas morning or your birthday parties. I may miss out on a fair amount of the day to day because of my work schedule, but I will never let the work get in the way of the big moments.

Life Gets Better And Better

Life gets better and better when you begin to live deliberately. When you choose your destiny instead of letting it (hopefully) find it's way to you. Make the decisions that will change your life and you'll attract the exact things you want into your life.

Happiness Comes From Inside

True happiness comes from inside you. It's part of a mindset. You can choose to be sad and bitter over things, or you can choose to be happy. Obviously it's better and far more enjoyable to choose to be happy. It's not always easy to get to the point where you're truly happy, but the more you work at it and the more you realize when you're not there, getting there becomes easier.

Be Present In Relationships

Be there in the moment, actively live your life with other people. It's far too easy to get lost, focus on other things and lose sight of why you're here on earth. Focus. That one word will pull it all together for you. Focus on the people that matter to you. Focus on growing those relationships. Focus on giving back to those people. Focus on the life you want.

....

"I've learned that people will forget what you said, people will forget what you did, but people will never forget how you made them feel." - Maya Angelou

....

Music

Let music move you and inspire you to do great things. Every once in a while you'll hear a song that just grabs you, captivates you and inspires you to do great things. Go with that feeling, you'll find incredible things hidden behind music that you love.

As a kid, I thought I hated music. Every time we went somewhere in the car, we would listen to the radio or a tape (I'll have to explain what those are to you, haha), and inevitably it was something my sisters loved. I always thought the headaches I got were a result of music, when in reality it was probably more car sickness and bright sunlight. But there's a good chance that the music was as awful as being car sick in a hot car too.

Now that I'm older, I've come to really understand that you have to find the music that you love, that speaks to the core of who you are. Don't necessarily follow what everyone else is listening to if it isn't what really resonates with you.

The Happiness Of Your Life

....
"The happiness of your life depends on the quality of your thoughts."
– Marcus Aurelius
....

What you decide to put into your mind and bring into your life is what will take hold and grow. People that choose to surround themselves with negativity and bad things will tend to receive those things. And likewise, those that choose optimism, and happiness will tend to receive those things.

Intentionally choose to think positive thoughts and you'll find yourself happier with little effort.

Friendship

I've had a lot of friends come and go from my life, as you will with yours. That's intentional, they aren't all meant to be a part of our lives forever. That means you must value those friendships highly while you're in the midst of them. Spend time with these people, have fun, laugh and create new experiences.

Finding good friends gets harder as you age and things begin to get in the way. Jobs, people moving away, family, volunteer commitments and people trying to achieve their own dreams. It's easy to put your friends in the back of your mind and you'll surely drift to the back of theirs as well. Try not to let that happen, it's far easier to maintain good friendships than it is to find new ones. You will be busy, and there will be a lot on your mind, make sure one of those things is your friends, and make the time to see them.

There's a common saying that you're the sum of the 5 people you spend the most time with. It's very true. Surround yourself with motivated people that are striving for great things in their life. Their efforts and passion will automatically bring you up a level. Avoid people that are stumbling through life and aren't motivated to pursue greatness, they'll only drag you down a level.

> "The trouble is not in dying for a friend, but in finding a friend worth dying for."
> – Mark Twain

Make time to continue to grow and enjoy your friendships. As you get older, you'll have a lot of things thrown your way, work, kids, chores, on and on. Don't let those things get in the way of maintaining friendships or growing new ones. I've made far too many excuses in my life for not having the friendships that I wanted to have. Don't make excuses. Invest that time and energy into your friends instead.

Explore The World

Get out there and visit the world. If you love cities, go to cities and explore. If you love nature like I do, then get outside to the wild places that inspire you. There's so much more going on in the world than what's immediately in front of us and our daily lives. We miss out on far too much getting sucked into these monotonous and reoccurring lifestyles and we forget to explore the world and everything it has to offer except on a few brief occasions we like to call vacations.

Time For Yourself

Take time to be alone. It's important to be by yourself, reflect, take time to think and not be concerned about everyone else in the world, even if it's just for a few minutes each day. That time alone will help you to clear your mind of all the clutter. A practice that is well worth the few minutes it takes.

Make Time

Make time for the ones you love. In your life you'll often find yourself saying "I don't have the time." That's just an excuse that we all love to tell ourselves and others. We're all given 24 hours in a day, some choose to use those hours more wisely than others. Make the right choice. You can always make time and clear useless things from your schedule for the people you care most about. And big tip, one of those people should be yourself. Find the time to work on improving your life, every single day.

The Magic Of The Moment

Life is an amazing journey, we're all blessed with some pretty incredible things while we're figuring out what it means to be alive. Don't miss those moments. Be present. Be engaged and enjoy them. By far the best moments I've experienced have been the births of my boys, but there are so many other moments that are right up there.

Many people call it mindfulness or being present, call it whatever you want, but just be there. Be in that specific moment you're experiencing and take it all in. As kids, we are all single focused, enjoying the moment we're in, rarely paying any attention to the future. While we can't live that way all the time as productive adults, it's necessary to fully appreciate the good things in life.

It's hard to describe the feeling you get when you're watching life unfold in all it's incredible ways. Watching your kids run around like crazy and enjoying every minute of it. Don't get so caught up in the bigger picture that you forget to pay attention to all the details that make that picture so awesome.

Do Something Spontaneous

Do something spontaneous. Someone will come up with a crazy idea, sometimes you just need to say yes. We were visiting a friend at UCONN, late on a Wednesday night when someone proposed the idea that we should go to New York City to Times Square. So we crammed into a tiny pickup truck and set out for the city. When we got there, we saw a lonely horse and carriage guy, so we piled in and went for a ride.

Was it pointless? Perhaps. But sometimes the journey and the story you create is all that matters.

Make Someone Else Truly Happy

Think beyond yourself. Make someone else truly happy. I love the feeling I get from making someone else happy. It's way more rewarding than just seeking out things for myself. In some small way, you know you made their life better. And whether you believe in Karma or not, that goodness will come back to you at some point.

Go Confidently

....

"Go confidently in the direction of your dreams. Live the life you've imagined."

– Henry David Thoreau

....

That Feeling When You Know It's Just Right

Appreciate that feeling you get when you know something is just right, or it's meant to be. It's not a feeling you can fully describe, but you'll know when it hits you.

When we got Dallas (our golden retriever for those not in the know), I drove up to Holyoke, Massachusetts with your aunt Danielle and Sam, the lady brought the puppies out and Dallas immediately came up to Danielle and laid down. We knew right away that she was the puppy for our family and we never looked back.

There was never a doubt in our minds that we picked the right dog. Knowing for certain that something is just meant to be, and never having to think twice about it, well that's when you know you're in the zone.

Smile

Remember to smile. But more importantly, smile when you're feeling down, it will instantly lift your spirits. It's nearly impossible to smile and be grumpy, so smile away.

....

"Wrinkles should merely indicate where smiles have been."

– Mark Twain

....

Have Fun
Have fun with friends, by yourself or with your family. Laugh often. Create memories. Enjoy experiences. Do things that make you nervous. But most of all, have fun.

Let The Inconsequential Things Go
Learn to let the inconsequential things go. There are many things in life that are worth fighting for, and there are many, many more things that aren't worth the stress, frustration, time and anger to fight over. You'll find yourself happier, more decisive and easier to get along with.

....
"It's perfectly alright to fall madly in love with Life."
– Jesse Elder
....

The 10 Happiest Moments Of My Life
1. When my first son Benjamin was born. It was the single most exciting and scary moment I've ever experienced. I don't cry often, but I'll fully admit that I did on that day.
2. When my second son Matthew was born. I was so excited to grow our family again.
3. Buying our first home shortly after Ben was born.
4. My first real relationship, she was a great person and we had some amazing times. Cherish those moments when you first fall truly, deeply in love with someone.
5. The first structure fire I fought interior on. There was an adrenaline rush that I had never before felt.

6. Camping: I'll lump these into one category, but I loved camping as a kid so every day was special.
7. The day I moved out of the house and my father stopped me and told me how proud he was of me and everything I've accomplished. He's not one to say those things often, so it meant a lot to me.
8. Every time I help to save a life. I don't recall the very first life I saved, but that doesn't matter. What matters is that every time I pick up that phone and help someone do CPR and we bring someone back, there's a massive overwhelm that you just did something awesome.
9. Hiking to the top of Mt. Washington. We were ill prepared for what a mountain would throw at us, little water, little food and no gear. But we made it. Conquering my first real mountain was a major triumph and the views were simply amazing.
10. Stepping out of my comfort zone and coming out with a win. I know, this is pretty generic, but every time I do something that makes me nervous and I succeed, that's an amazing feeling. I know now that I can do it and it builds my confidence level up every time.

Take Vacations

Escape from reality, if only for a moment at a time. Taking vacations is one of the best ways to reset your mind and to get back to what life is really all about. There have been years at a time where I've just kept on chugging, never stopping for a break. That wears you down.

Escape your daily grind and go see the places that you want to explore. I guarantee you'll walk away a happier person and with more memories too. Nobody looks back fondly on the times they spent working 16 hour days for months straight, no, they look back and remember the vacations, the moments with their families and friends.

Don't Wait

Don't wait until time is short to live out your wildest dreams. By then, it may be too late to fully experience them.

Revolving

Your life should never revolve around your work. It should revolve around your family, your friends, your experiences and everything great that life brings. Work is simply a part of the equation. As you grow up, you will have to devote a fair amount of your life to it, but it shouldn't become your every waking moment. And if you follow my guidance along the way, your work will be something you're passionate about, at least on some level, so those hours you devote to working won't be all that bad.

You Have The Power To Be Happy

I've seen a lot of people walking around in a constant miserable state in my life. In fact, I've been one at many times. It's way too easy to get wrapped up in life's issues and to let them get the better of you.

You have the power to choose to be happy. To choose a life and a mindset that brings happiness to your life and those around you. Use your power, use it every chance you get. It's far better to be known as the guy that's always happy versus the guy that's always miserable.

Start Living Today

    Start Truly Living Today. Not tomorrow. Not next week or next month. Start truly living your life today. And then keep at it each and every day.

....

"Life is short, Break the Rules.
Forgive quickly, Kiss SLOWLY.
Love truly. Laugh uncontrollably
And never regret ANYTHING
That makes you smile."
- Mark Twain

....

Part Six:
Personal Growth

Becoming The Best Version Of Yourself

Personal growth... Oh where to get started? Here's the thing. Whether you focus on it intentionally or not, your entire life is going to revolve around your growth.

The best way you can make massive leaps in your personal growth is to be devoted to it. To focus your energy and mindset on constantly getting yourself to the next level. You'll continue to grow whether you choose to focus on it or not, but it will come faster and far more directed if you do focus on it. I fell in love with personal growth shortly after you were born. I realized I was going to have to create some massive changes in my life to really live the life that I wanted to have, and that I wanted you to have.

I began seeking out resources, people I could follow, books to read, audio programs to listen to because I knew that would help guide me to the next level. Some things I've done have been more successful than others, but every little bit towards the bigger picture is what matters.

I talk about the compounding effect in the last section of this book, and while it applies to nearly everything in life, it's especially important for your personal growth. Everything you work towards builds on top of the other things you've already worked on, adding up and up, and increasing the rate at which you succeed. And when you see yourself making massive gains in your personal life and towards your own goals, you can't help but be excited about the process.

Be Mindful Of What You Consume

We live in an era where there's more information coming at us in a single day than most of humanity would have been hit with in a lifetime. Be mindful of what you're consuming as content and how much of it. It's nice to relax and watch tv from time to time, but it shouldn't become a cornerstone of your life. Use it as a specific tool to relax or watch something you're interested in, when that show is over, turn it off so it doesn't suck you in and take over your life.

Be aware of the types of information that are coming your way, and remember, you control the input. Pay attention to positive things that are going to move you forward in life, avoid the drama and negativity that abounds. The only output you can receive is derived from what you're putting into your system. So if you constantly feed it with negative, petty things, that's the best you're going to get out. Instead, fill your life with inspiration, happiness and experiences and you'll live a much more fulfilled life.

Confidence

I've struggled with confidence for the majority of my life. I think it mostly ties back to the fact that I'm an introvert and relatively shy. It's weird though because it only pops up in certain aspects of my life, while others, I can walk around like I'm the king of the castle.

If you're ever struggling with confidence, take a second to analyze what you're up against. Do you have the skills to complete the task at hand? If yes, then just get it done. It won't get any easier to doubt yourself or postpone getting it done. In fact, the best way to overcome confidence problems is to continually put yourself in those situations where you feel the most vulnerable, when you successfully complete it, you'll instantly get a boost of confidence that will endure the next time you're faced with the same problem.

If you don't have the skills to complete what you're up against, you have three options. First, try to figure it out and get through it. Doing this can be incredibly valuable since you'll learn something in the process and you'll gain confidence to tackle other new things when they come your way.

Your second option is to stop what you're doing and learn the skill. That option has its pros and cons, it could take years to learn the skill or just minutes, that's something you'll have to weigh at the time.

And the third option is to outsource it. If it's a skill that you'll use once in your life, it's probably faster and easier to outsource the job to someone else that has the skills to get it done.

I know a lot of men want to be the kind of guy that can do everything. Well, I'm here to tell you that's crazy. You can't know everything in the world, and there are a lot of things that aren't worth investing your time or energy in to figure out how to do when people who are experts can easily be hired to do it for you. It's a fine balance between what your time is worth and what it will cost you to get it done.

Connect With Nature

Find a way to spend time in nature, and do it as frequently as possible. You'll be more grounded, relaxed and in tune with the world. I know, I know, that sounds like a hippie talking, but it's true. Take a look at someone who lives in the city, spends all of their time there and works like crazy and you'll see exactly what I'm talking about.

They're beaten down and nowhere near as excited about life and experiencing everything they possibly can while they're here. Our time is short here, regardless of how long it may feel at times. So you need to take control of your life and remain balanced.

Your mother and I are both mountains and lake people, grandma on the other hand loves the ocean. I don't care what place motivates you the most or you feel most connected to, but find one and spend time there. Only by doing that will you truly understand the power of what I'm talking about here. It's incredibly difficult to explain what you need to learn by connecting with nature, but trust me, get out there and do it, you'll understand and you'll thank me.

Disconnect From Technology

I miss the days when we weren't so connected. Don't get me wrong, I love having so much information and entertainment at my fingertips, but it's a constant distraction. Rather than just using it here and there, I find myself constantly on it as a way to kill time. That's some damn valuable time that I'm losing though. I could be doing a million other things like learning, reading, writing or creating instead.

I'm working hard, and hopefully by the time you read this and understand what I'm saying, I will be far more disconnected to the world than I am connected. It all has it's places, but I think to really create and have true connections with people, we all need to disconnect from the digital world more often and get back to living.

I can tell you with 100% confidence that the best moments in my life all occurred digital free. Moments where I was truly living in the moment and taking in the world around me. Like the day you and your brother were born, hiking Mount Washington, and kayaking through rapids in Quebec. Yes, I had phones and was communicating with people after those experiences, but certainly not in the middle. I was there and couldn't care less about what was being posted online or the emails that were coming in.

Try that, challenge yourself to disconnect more often and live a life full of actual hands on, life shocking, memory making, amazing and unforgettable moments. Or just take that time to simply be, either way, you'll open your life up to far better things than a cell phone or tablet can do for you.

Don't Compare Yourself To Others

Don't compare yourself to others. You're living a life that is uniquely you. Instead, be concerned with how you're living in the world. Are you compassionate, doing good things and providing value to others? That's the heart of what really matters, not whether you're making the same amount of money, as popular or famous as someone else. We're all on our own adventure in life, and working towards our own goals, don't mistake someone else's achievements for what you think you wanted.

It's good to aspire, dream big and admire the achievements of others but don't sell yourself short by comparing your life to theirs, your journey in life may have plans to bring you elsewhere and have major successes in other parts of your life than theirs has.

....

"You measure the size of the accomplishment by the obstacles you had to overcome to reach your goals."
— Booker T. Washington

....

Don't Complain

Oh boy do I have trouble with this one. I'm far from an angel when it comes to complaining, but hey, life is always a work in progress right?

So if I haven't perfected this one, why am I telling you not to do it?

Quite simply, nobody likes to listen to people complain. There are two types of people in life when it comes to complaining. There are those that sit there and complain, then do nothing about it. And then there are the people that complain, but get off their butt and do something about it.

I used to be a part of the first group, but over the last few years, I've shifted towards the latter. And that's the type of person I would prefer you to be. If you're going to complain about things (of course, I would prefer that you not complain at all and instead just get started on fixing the problems you find, but that's a topic for another time).

Life happens. You may lose your job, your car may break down, you may get mugged. It's all a part of learning and growing, and while there are lessons to be learned from those experiences themselves, the more powerful lessons will be learned when you determine how you'll respond to a situation.

You'll have two options when something happens in your life that you don't like. First, you can sit there like most people and complain about it to anyone that will listen. Or, you can get off your butt and find a solution to your problem.

You lost your job? Ok, get out there and find another one, or better yet, create your own job. Car broke down? Find a mechanic and get it fixed. Got mugged? What were you doing in the city anyways? You know we're country people, haha.

Remember, you are solely responsible for your success and failures in life. So if you want to sit back and complain but not do anything, that is your option. But the smarter thing to do is get up, get out there and tackle your issues head on.

Finding Your Way

The world is a great big place, it's easy to get lost in the shuffle of everything that's going on. To find your way, follow your passion, do good and you'll eventually arrive home. For me, that's always been about surrounding myself with nature and protecting the places that I enjoy spending most of my time in. It may be something entirely different for you, and that's ok, just find the things you love and follow those, they'll eventually lead you where you need to go.

....
"If a man knows not to which port he sails,
no wind is favorable."
– Seneca
....

Gratitude

This is a habit that I developed sometime around 2012. It really began because I was trying so hard to change my life, to get out of my job and develop an entrepreneurial mind set. I read somewhere about a few habits to get into, one of those was creating a daily to do list (I'll write more about that later).

But expressing gratitude was another major component of that. I keep it incredibly simple, because simple works and there's no need to overcomplicate this. All I do is write down 3 things that I'm grateful for that day. That's it.

Some days it's because you did something funny or made me laugh, other times when someone like grandma helps us out with watching you and your brother, and yet other times, I'm just thankful for all the beauty and nature around us.

Doing this has changed my thinking, big time. Now instead of just trying to get through every day, I take time to notice the world around me. I'm constantly on the lookout for things that make me appreciate all of the great things I have in my life.

This is a daily habit for me. It's become a MUST DO. And it was easy to implement because it's so damn simple and I get an immediate benefit (happiness) out of doing it.

Go ahead, grab a journal and try it out. You'll see a massive change in the way you think and I bet you'll appreciate life more, even if it's just little by little.

I'm Not Saying It's Going To Be Easy

"I'm not saying it's going to be easy, I'm saying it's going to be worth it"

This is an incredibly powerful quote. I have no idea who said it, but it resonates to my core. When I saw it online, my immediate thought process was to just keep on going through the quotes and reading them mindlessly, but then in an instant it struck a chord with me.

I realized that everything I've been pushing myself for over the last few years hasn't always made sense. I've been frustrated and tired. It's been a struggle in almost every way. Sometimes I wish I could go back to the way life was before where I didn't worry about making myself a better person, or getting to the next level. Life was still frustrating then, but it was easier. I didn't worry as much about progress and getting to a peak level.

And an easier life is what we're all after right? Because that comfort zone is our goal, it's a natural place to want to settle into.

Well I used to be that way. I always looked for the easiest route, or the simplest so I wouldn't have to put in a lot of effort, but that was the old me. Now I'm on this journey of personal growth, business development and achieving such incredible things that there's no way I could turn around.

Life isn't always easy, and it shouldn't be because that would cheat all of us out of what it means to be alive. So when you're faced with stress, frustration, fear of failure, exhaustion, etc, keep on pushing yourself. Keep pushing and striving towards your goals because that's where the real power lies. The people that achieve the greatest things in life are the ones that never give in, they keep working harder and harder to reach their goals because they know at the end of the day it will all be worth it.

....
"Motivation is what gets you started.
Habit is what keeps you going."
– Jim Ryun
....

Invest In Yourself

The single best investment you can ever make will be in yourself. It will always pay dividends far greater than those you could receive doing anything else.

Take classes, but take the classes you're interested in. Buy personal development programs or attend seminars – but focus on the areas you want to improve within yourself.

Do the things you enjoy doing – Don't spend time on hobbies or tasks that you don't enjoy, find a passion area and learn everything you can about that area.

I love personal development, but you have to be careful with it. When you finally come to the conclusion that you need to mindfully work on yourself every single day, it's going to consume you. Now, hopefully that's in a good way, and hopefully you'll be making such radical progress over time that it will be all worth it, but don't ever make changes and 'improvements' that aren't congruent with who you are.

It's easy to see someone rich, powerful and an expert in their field and to think you want to be just like them, but would it be worth it if to become that, you had to lose everything that defined who you are? My guess would be probably not.

Life Is A Video Game

I got this idea online from Steve Kamb, but I love the concept of it. I grew up playing video games with my friends. The original Nintendo came out when we were kids, then the systems took off from there. I remember spending hour upon hour playing a single game with my friends. It was exciting because these games and the systems were all at the breaking edge of technology at the time. But video games can become a powerful model to emulate.

When you look at the core of a game experience, you're constantly trying to take your character or team and level them up. In your life, you should be doing the exact same thing. You should constantly be working on improving yourself and getting to the next major point in life.

These characters also go off on epic adventures, I think you should do the same thing. Get out and explore the world for everything it has to offer. Find things that motivate you or you want to know more about and instead of just reading about them online, get out there and interact with them first hand. If you want to see the lava fields of Hawaii, find a way to get there and witness them first hand. If you want to become a better leader, find a way to get in charge of a group of people and do it.

I want to always encourage you to live a life that you'd be excited to tell people about and that they would be excited to hear about. Follow your true self first though and do the things that make you wake up every day and say 'hell yeah, let's get started.' I can't tell you how many days

I've woken up dreading getting started because I wasn't following a life that was exciting and truly me. Don't make the same mistake.

Take your character, set him off on an epic adventure of life and level up along the way.

Mistakes

You're going to make mistakes in this life. Most of them will be small, but occasionally you'll make big ones. And you know what? That's ok. It's a part of living and learning how to be human. I highly doubt that life was ever intended to be an easy journey. We have it much better in The United States than most countries around the world, but it's still not an easy world to live in.

I've never been proud or excited to make mistakes, I think I'd be crazy if I were. But as I grow older, I've been able to realize that every time I've screwed up in this life, I've been able to take a lesson from it. Most of the time I didn't make a conscious thought about what I was taking away, but on the rare occasion, I was so dumbfounded by my mistake that I couldn't help but think about it for a long time.

And as things go, the longer we think about them, the more reflection we have and the more we can take away lessons from them.

I've made some really stupid mistakes, like the time I thought I would build my own fort in the woods next to the house, I was using hedge clippers on a slope. I slipped and my thumb sliced open like a ragged edge of a metal can. Damn that was painful, but you bet I learned that I couldn't defy gravity with sharp metal objects!

Other mistakes I've made were much more heartfelt. I'll write more about these later, but I can tell you that mistakes in relationships are some of the most painful mistakes you will ever make. There are many things I regret saying, doing and things I intentionally avoided that I shouldn't have, all of which would have led to better relationships.

Mistakes are what they are. They aren't intentional, and often are a result of just being human. You're learning and growing, and making mistakes is one of the best methods to do that. It's logical that any mistake you make, if you take note of it, you aren't likely to make that same mistake again.

That's why making mistakes is ok. You should be able to develop new skill sets from them and avoid making those same mistakes over and over again.

You'll never stop making mistakes in your lifetime. But there's hope that if you continue to act intelligently and learn from your mistakes that you'll make fewer and fewer as you get older, but you're not infallible, NOBODY is.

On Shyness

I was a shy kid. I wasn't always that way though. When I was little, like you are now (2-3), there are reports of me being dancing machine. Anywhere, anytime there was music, I'd be out there dancing, regardless of who was watching.

I have no idea what happened that caused the shift. Perhaps I suddenly became aware of how big of a fool I looked like running around thinking I was dancing? Who really knows? But as I got older, I stepped away from the spotlight and did my own thing.

I wasn't the kind of freak that boarded up my windows and never went outside, but I was definitely the kid that took a lot of guts to put myself out there to meet new people.

It was sort of an odd mix really. I've always been shy around strangers and people I didn't really know well. But where it gets weird is that if I know you, even fairly well, I'll let you in on a lot of things that others may not readily talk about.

I consider myself a pretty open book. If you want to know something, most of the time you just have to ask and I'd be happy to share it with you. I'm not really sure why I'm this way, but it seems to be working pretty well, so I'll keep on chugging.

So how did I really begin to get over being shy?

Well it wasn't the easiest journey for me, but I wouldn't really consider it too difficult either. When I was 16, it took quite a bit of courage, but through the prodding of my best friend Rich, I joined the fire department. I was as nervous as could be about it. I mean who was I, a quiet 16 year old to join fire department and help save lives?

Over time though, I realized how much I fit in to an environment like that. It's almost like a wolf pack. There's a pecking order that naturally falls into place in an organization like that. Yes there are people with rank, but you'll often find that they aren't the most influential people in the organization. I felt at home.

And when I feel comfortable and at home, I'm not afraid to voice my opinion. There became a lot of opportunities to voice my opinion, but also my experience.

When I became a dispatcher, people often looked to me for guidance on how they should operate on the radio. When people begin to look to you for expertise, even if you don't feel like you are the 'guru', you immediately get to pump up your chest and spout off about everything you know.

And I'll be damned if that doesn't put some confidence into your step. Regardless of what it is in your life, when people begin to seek you out as an expert in something, or look for your guidance, it gives you an immediate boost. It's not something you can easily fake either, so it's important that it comes naturally if you're trying to make this an organic process.

That boost of confidence really pushed me to get over my shyness in a big way. There were plenty of senior members in the department, guys and gals that had 30 or more years of firefighting experience coming to me for answers at just 18 or 19 years old. It felt great, and it helped me build my confidence quickly.

The reality is that there's no reason to be shy. Everyone in this world is going through the same journey, learning how to be a human and finding their way. Everyone has doubts, fears and insecurities about themselves, don't trust someone if they tell you they don't, because they're lying.

I didn't learn that last part until a couple of years ago as I really began my major personal growth journey, but it's so incredibly important to understand. When you're able to understand that even the world's most successful and powerful people have had personal doubts, yet they managed to achieve everything they set after, how could you let your shyness keep you from achieving the same success?

I'm still working on overcoming parts of my shyness syndrome, but like anything else in this life, it's a work in progress. If it were as easy as whistling for a magic fairy to come grant a wish to make those feelings go away, there would be no value in growing as a person. I'll take each step one foot at a time and maybe occasionally one giant leap, but sooner or later I will get there.

Perfect Timing

You can't plan perfect timing.

I've tried many, many times to plan things for exactly the right time. And yes, everything from my education to planning you and your brother. Some things I needed to tackle to try and move my life ahead, others because I thought they were the right thing to do. No matter how much planning you do, there will be kinks thrown into your plan, things you never thought to anticipate. And those very things are going to throw off your so called 'perfect timing'.

So my advice to you? Just get started on whatever it is you want to accomplish. If it's meant to be the perfect time, it shall be, if not, that's ok, you'll figure out the problems and work your way through them.

The heart of the real matter here is that you just need to get started. Don't put off doing something in your life because it's not the perfect time. The perfect time seems to be something that just happens, and rarely to almost never because someone planned it to happen.

You'll find more and more throughout your life that when you seize opportunities that are presented to you, that those things will turn into the perfect timing.

Read

 Read voraciously. I never got into reading as a kid. I would pick up a book here and there and those I read, I usually did enjoy. But reading was never pushed in our home growing up. It was never discouraged, but I think we were always so busy, especially my father and I with hockey that it just didn't end up on the high priority list of things they wanted us to focus on. Fortunately or unfortunately for you, it will be in ours.

 Why?

 Because reading opens up new worlds to you. Whether you read stories of people slaying dragons or books about starting your own business, you're expanding your mind and your ability to think. It's not something you can acquire from watching hours of television.

 Because of that, your mother and I are trying to instill amazing habits of reading by making it a daily habit at bed time. And so far, you're loving it. I love to see you get excited about racing me to your book shelf to be able to pick a book for story time. Sometimes I beat you there, sometimes you beat me, but I always let you pick the story anyways.

 So I don't care what you read, just read. And make it a daily habit.

....

 "Don't just say you have read books. Show that through them you have learned to think better, to be a more discriminating and reflective person. Books are the training weights of the mind. They are very helpful, but it would be a bad mistake to suppose that one has made progress simply by having internalized their contents."

- Epictetus

....

Solving Problems

The world is full of problems, some are created by nature, most by man. You can gain a lot of value and power in this world if you can figure out how to solve those problems for people. Don't be the kind of person that creates more problems, instead, be on the constant look out for problems you can solve and then get to work solving them. The world will reward you handsomely when you do that.

Struggling

Even as I write this book, I'm struggling with things in life. I want desperately to get out of my 'day job' as a 911 dispatcher. It's not that I don't enjoy the work, I'm just done with it. I've accomplished a lot, but there's no further room for upward movement. Sitting in a dead end job sucks. Sure, the pay is ok, but when you realize that just going in to work every day for the next forty years is it, well, that sucks.

It's not inspiring, it's not motivating and it isn't helping me to push myself to new levels. I don't want to be the type of person that just bums along in a job until I'm too old to read my own name on a computer screen so I have to retire. That's just not the way the world has to work anymore, so there's no reason to keep going that route.

The hardest part to wanting to get out of my job is that I have no clue exactly what I want to be when I grow up. I've thought about running away to the circus, but my feet just aren't big enough for clown shoes. But in reality, when you finally decide to take life into your hands, not the hands of your boss or company, it's a massive mind shift.

I'm afraid. If I fail, is my safety net big enough to catch me? I've always sat in a nice little comfort zone. More money coming in than going out, guaranteed paycheck every two weeks. It's a nice life. It's easy to sit back and not have to worry about running a business and getting new sales all the time. In fact, I'm in the best job if that were the life I was seeking. People come to me when they need something, and I'm not judged on the amount of activity I generate since I can't reasonably generate any activity. It's all reactive.

Back to that fear. That fear paralyzes decision making processes. There are plenty of things I could go do, but I'm at this point where I really want to have a location independent lifestyle so I can spend more time with my family and friends. But what can I do that will provide a lot more money than I'm making now and still provide me with the lifestyle I'm desperately after?

I battle with these thoughts every single day. It's mind numbing at times because I feel like I've been working at this for 3 years now, with little results to show for it. But the reason I have little results to show for it is because I've failed to take action.

Ben, the world rewards people that take action. Whether it's the entirely right move or not, that doesn't matter. If you're moving forward, you can at least correct your course for where you need to go. But if you sit back on your heals, waiting and waiting for that perfect moment to come to you, you'll never get there.

Sometimes you just have to trust your gut, go for it and push yourself through the wall so you can get started.

There will be times in your life when you're struggling. It may be because of your job, housing, love or any variety of things. The best advice I can give you when you're facing those moments is to take the time truly think about what you're up against.

When you take that time, you can come up with a variety of options to overcome almost any problem you're faced with. Actually, while you're at that, come up with 10 solid ideas for any problem you face. If the first one fails you, then you can easily shift your focus to another solution.

Having ten times the backup to any problem you may face will mean you don't have to slow down. You can keep pushing yourself further and harder than anyone around you is willing to go. When you do that, you can almost guarantee your success.

Take Care Of Your Body

Just like your mind, you're given just one body in this life. I'm guilty of neglecting this rule as are many that read this book. While I generally pay attention to what I'm putting in and what I do to my body, I've rarely in my life take then time to make sure my body is a finely tuned instrument.

Why does all of that matter? To keep it simple. This is your one shot. This is the one attempt you have at living an awesome life. And to live your awesome life, you need the ability to do things, which happen through the use of your body.

Your mind, your body and your soul are all tied together. Take care of each of them and they will take care of you.

Take Care Of Your Mind

Learn. Experience. Live. You're given only one life on this planet, make it everything you can. Invest in knowledge and expand your mind beyond what you're always used to. Read books, go to seminars, create mastermind groups, do creative thinking your way. I encourage you to find any way you can to expand your mind and ability to think. I love laying down in bed with you as we read bed time stories and then putting the books down to create our own stories from our imaginations. You're hilarious when you tell me about a racecar "Goes like this" as you zoom your arm across and say "Real Fast!"

It's easy to let your mind go into a vegetative state where you never really use it. You no longer create or aspire to big things. Don't let that happen. The world is out there waiting for everything you can possibly create and throw its way. The more you do it, the better it gets and the more freeing it is. So learn the things you want to learn about. Explore the places you want to explore. And live the life that you truly want to live, because it's through doing these things that you truly take care of your mind, your body and your soul.

Know Where You're Going

Know where you're going. You can't get very far if you're forever heading down the wrong path towards the wrong goals. I know it's difficult to figure out exactly what you want and where you should take your life. I've struggled for years at a time trying to figure that out. I sat in the same stagnant job counting the minutes on the clock, working nights, weekends, holidays and missing out on the most important parts of life because I didn't know where I wanted to go in life.

It's vital to take the time you need to figure out your life. Your journey may change several times over the course of your life, but the key is that you're on a well-defined path to a known destination at each step of the way.

Think about it this way. You venture off for a hike in the woods. You're going to bring a map with you. As you journey along your chosen path, you know exactly where you're heading and where you will arrive. You may come across other trails along the way and decide to venture down them to experience something new or pursue a different course, but you still know exactly where you're going and what's at the end of the trail because you have your map and you've spent time learning the area you're putting yourself into. It's the same as investing in yourself to figure out where you really want to go.

Plan

Your life is totally in your control, you can take it wherever you want it to go, so make sure you don't just let it happen to you. What you should be doing is continually making plans for where you want to be in life so you can work towards them. You may shift and adjust your plans, but without a plan in place, you're relying on someone else to create your future for you.

>"The reason most people never reach their goals is that they don't define them, or ever seriously consider them as believable or achievable. Winners can tell you where they are going, what they plan to do along the way, and who will be sharing the adventure with them."
>
>– Denis Watiley

Get To Know Your Family

Spend time learning about your family and your heritage. I never really invested the time to get to know some of the people in my life, and I regret that quite often because I'm sure they would have had quite a bit of wisdom to pass on to me, and great stories.

Getting to know your heritage will help you stay grounded to what this life is really all about. You didn't simply become because your mom and I got together. There's centuries of life beyond us that caused all of this to become a reality.

An Oak Tree

An oak tree is a very powerful being. It has the ability to shade you, drink up excess water, provide oxygen and shelter and when you chop it down, it can keep you warm. And yet it asks for nothing in return except a clean, healthy environment to grow and thrive in to provide you all of this. Is that too much to ask?

You Are Powerful

You are an incredibly powerful person. You don't need anyone to affirm that for you. You hold all the courage you will ever need, figure out how to release it and then harness it for your own success.

....

"You have power over your mind-not outside events. Realize this and you will find strength."
    - Marcus Aurelius

....

Invest In Yourself

Invest in growing yourself. Buy books, videos, training courses, go to seminars. Whatever it takes to grow and nurture yourself to the next level, do it. We're all on an incredible journey in life, but it's not a journey we can figure out entirely by ourselves. Follow the people that inspire you and motivate you. Dismiss those that discourage you or dissuade you.

Take Time For yourself

Take time for yourself. Take time alone to think and figure yourself out. No distractions, no outside influences, just yourself. Reflect, plan and grow during this time. It's in these moments that we often see our biggest gains.

Don't Allow Your Mind to Be Still

Don't allow your mind to be still for long. It's always good to relax and refocus ourselves, but we need to consistently push our minds to be able to continue to grow.

An idle mind opens itself to the ideals of others, which may not be in tune with one's own plans and life design.

Clear Past Conditioning

Clear your mind of past conditioning. When you begin to transform your life, there will be barriers in the way, often coming in the form of prior life conditioning (experiences, education, jobs, relationships, etc). Those barriers must first be broken through to be able to push yourself to the next level. If you fail to do that, and you're trying to make changes in your life that contradict everything you are familiar with, you'll face a lot of internal resistance.

People are often concerned about outside influences limiting their ability to become who they want to be. I've found that the greatest limitations in my life actually have come from myself and almost never from outside influences. Often referred to as 'head trash', these are the very things that limit your ability to achieve all of the things you want in life. It's all bs though, it's contrived thoughts in your head that don't mean anything other than the meaning you give to them.

People love to tell you something can't be done simply because they never did it themselves or never saw it done. You'll have to defy them and your current mindset if you're going to achieve big things.

Stiffest Tree

"Notice that stiffest tree is most easily cracked, while the bamboo or willow survives by bending with the wind." - Bruce Lee

Be flexible, bend when the wind blows in your direction and you'll be able to withstand far more than most people.

Indecision

"The reason people are seemingly distracted all the time or seemingly indecisive all the time overwhelmed with 30 things they could be doing is because their goals are impotent.... The goals they have aren't exciting enough to compel them to take one direction or choose one thing." - Tim Ferriss

Making Decisions

....
"The more decisive person always wins."
- Chris Lockwood
....

When your mind comes to a decision, that should be it. You should take immediate action on it, or if that's not possible, at least stop debating your options. A decision should be a firm commitment to yourself to get it done. Too often in life we teeter back and forth between all of our options, and never end up committing to anything. I've been there far too often in my life, and I've wasted a lot of mental resources debating between things that really didn't matter much.

....
"You never really made a decision if you go back on it." - Chris Lockwood
....

Thirst For Knowledge

You should have an unquenchable thirst for knowledge. Always pursuing new information, learning about things that excite you or engage your mind. It doesn't always matter if there's an immediate use for it. It could spark new ideas that could revolutionize your life, and that's what's so awesome about learning.

....

"Education is the most powerful weapon which we can use to change the world."
- Nelson Mandela

....

Keep An Open Mind

Keep an open mind about things. Everything is not always black and white, there's a lot of color to the world, and closing your mind to only certain thoughts and ideas will void those colors from your spectrum. That's the problem I have with religions, so many of them close people's minds into thinking and doing certain things that people miss out on so many opportunities to see life in other ways. This isn't about religion per say, it was just an example, but it illustrates the idea. Just because something is different to you doesn't necessarily make it right or wrong, it may just be that you don't know enough about it yet.

Facing Down Your Fears

We all have fears, some rational, so many more that are completely irrational. I've always been afraid of open heights. I can fly in airplanes, be in tall buildings, none of that bothers me, but being in a situation where I could easily fall seems to get to me. Sounds crazy considering I'm a firefighter, I know. But I get by. I'll do ladder work if I have to, but I'd much prefer to go interior on a hose line.

So how do you overcome a fear, especially one like heights, where it's an ever present danger? The best advice I have for you is to face it head on. I willingly put myself onto roofs when the opportunity presents itself and I can more easily control the situation. And over the years, my fear has subsided quite a bit.

Facing your fears when you can control the outcome makes it easier to control the emotions that rise up in the heat of the moment. Let's say you were afraid of snakes, going to animal handler and having them teach you about them, show you how to hold them and guiding you into it would greatly reduce your anxiety about snakes. You'll begin to know why they do the things they do and what you can expect from them. Next time you stumble upon one in the woods, you won't be quite as afraid since you'll have knowledge you can use in that situation.

It works for anything in your life, not just wild animals. Face your fears head on, learn about what causes them to be a fear for you, and learn how you can get around them. Being forever afraid of something won't help you progress in life, and that's what we're all about, consistent progress.

....

"People have a hard time letting go of their suffering. Out of a fear of the unknown, they prefer suffering that is familiar."
– Thich Nhat Hanh

....

Obsessing

....

"Obsessing over things we cannot change robs us of the possibility of investing in the things we can."
- Johnathan Fields

....

Never Give Up On This

"Face your fears. Become the person you need to become in order to achieve the goals and dreams you want to achieve. Control what you can, cope with what you can't, and concentrate on what counts. Never give up on what is important to you...but make sure you know what that is." - Craig Ballantyne

Mindfulness

Practice mindfulness. Be aware of what's happening around you. Strive to appreciate amazing moments as they're happening. They're never as clear or vivid as they are in the present moment.

Sheep Dog

In your life, you should aim to be the sheep dog, not the sheep. Be the one leading, guiding and protecting the flock. The sheep are influenced by the actions of the dog. He guides them where they need to go and protects them when danger arises. We all start out as a sheep, we follow others actions, do as we're told and go with the pack. Slowly as we get older, some of the braver ones venture out and take on bigger and more powerful roles, while the others stay huddled up nice and safe in their flock, never pushing themselves to get better.

Don't be the one that sits there quietly in the middle of the flock feeling nice and safe. Push yourself out of your comfort zone and grow. Lead the flock to something bigger and better than status quo.

Starting Out Is Hard

When you're looking to make great strides in your life, you're going to come to a point where you realize now is the time. It's time to put your best foot forward and to leap into the life you need to have. It's tough to make that commitment to yourself. But the hard work really comes when you're in the middle of everything, pushing yourself to stay committed to the changes you want to make. Anybody can get started, but few will actually follow through long enough to see the results of what they began.

"The <u>first</u> steps toward wisdom are the most strenuous, because our weak and stubborn souls dread exertion (without absolute guarantee of reward) and the unfamiliar. As you progress in your efforts, your resolve is fortified and self-improvement progressively comes easier. By and by it actually becomes difficult to work counter to your own best interest.

By the steady but patient commitment to removing unsound beliefs from our souls, we become increasingly adept at seeing through flimsy fears, our bewilderment in love, and our lack of self-control. We stop trying to look good to others. One day, we contentedly realize we've stopped playing to the crowd." - Epictetus

Be True To Yourself

You're on a journey in this life, just like the rest of us. I wish there were a clear path that I could tell you to take and everything would turn out perfect, just like you'd always wanted. But life is never that easy. The surest advice I can give you (and advice I've ignored for a long time) is to be true to yourself. You know at your heart what the right move is for you.

As long as you're doing good things, there's no need to follow societies norms. Break free and follow your own path to the life you want to live. When everyone is zigging, you should zag. There's far more power in being the person that's following their passion and living a life they love than just being a mindless drone doing what you think is right by societies standards.

....

"Accomplishing someone else's goals doesn't mean your success." - Chris Lockwood

....

It Doesn't Get Easier

Life doesn't get any easier as you grow older. You'll always be faced with new and ever more complicated tasks to manage. The benefit is that the things that used to be difficult for you are now common place and simple to get around. Life is a challenge, I've said it before, but that's part of what makes life so worth living.

Consider The Other Side

Nearly everything you experience in life, someone else will also experience some aspect of it with you. Consider their side of things, their perception and their reactions. It's entirely possible, in fact, highly probable that their experience was perceived differently than your own, at least in some small way.

Single Best Investment

The single best investment I ever made was in myself, not a company.

Fully Experience Life

The only way to fully experience life is to get to know yourself. Know what motivates you, what drives you and what pushes you to be a better person. Most people drift through life fulfilling other people's dreams, handling 'emergencies' and never truly figuring themselves out. If they simply took time to figure out themselves, they wouldn't have to deal with all of those other things, thus living a more fulfilled life.

It's Easy To Put Up A Front

It's easy to put up a front to the public. To appear more successful, happier, or like you know everything that is thrown your way. But there's no fooling yourself, trying to only leads to delaying your success and ability to overcome your weaknesses. Be honest, be open and be yourself.

Guiding Principles

Create guiding principles for your life. A simple set of 10 to 12 should suffice. These guiding principles become what you base all of your decisions on. Instead of hemming and hawing when it comes time to make a decision, you simply validate it against your guiding principles. If it's in line with them, then go ahead with it, if not, let it go.

Some examples of my guiding principles are (in no particular order):
1. I will write everyday
2. I will work on my connections with my friends and family every day
3. I will devote time to my family every day
4. Life is about more than just me; I will help other people progress in their life too
5. Connect with nature – spend time outdoors, explore and learn about what's around me
6. My body is essential to my well-being
7. I will train my mind daily
8. Honesty is not negotiable
9. I will explore the world and fill my life with adventures both big and small
10. I will pursue my vision of a great life
11. I will give back to things that are important to me

These don't have to be your guiding principles, they are merely an example of what mine look like. They are fluid, don't be afraid to change them over time.

It's Ok To Go Backwards

Sometimes to move forward in life you need to take a few steps backwards, then realign yourself. As long as you don't stay at those backwards steps for long, it's ok to take them. But push yourself forward in a new direction. So many people look at taking a backwards step as a bad thing. When done properly, it can be the very best move you could make.

Starting Out

When you first start out on your own in life, there's a good chance it's going to be hard. You're going to have bills to pay, rent to cover, home furnishings to buy, etc. Know that you'll make it. You'll figure it out and get through the troubles.

Don't compare your life just starting out on your own to those who have been at it for decades, you're playing in a completely different league. They started where you are, and worked their way up. You'll do the same, it's just a matter of how quickly you make that happen through hard work and adding value to the world.

Part Seven:
What They Don't Teach You In School

Life's Lessons Aren't Always Taught In The Classroom

Pay attention long enough and you'll soon realize that most of life's best lessons aren't actually taught to you in the classroom. Yes, you will learn quite a bit and most of it will be useful at some point in your life, but there are so many more lessons to be learned through experiencing life.

This section of the book is going to cover a wider and albeit more unique variety of subjects that didn't seem to fit into any particular part of the rest of the book. I chose to include them because I think they're vital to your long term success.

While much of this segment is on building your wealth, reducing your debt and stabilizing your financial future, remember that these things weren't learned in a classroom. I learned these lessons either through personal experience or because I deliberately sought out the information I needed to be able to succeed in that area of my life.

I'm far from being a wealth master in my life, but I'm working towards it deliberately each and every day.

In your life, you will learn countless things in the traditional classroom environment. And that's a great place to start, but don't stop there. Follow your desires to learn more about things that interest you, that inspire you, that put you in a state of awe. A life filled with self-guided education will leave you far more fulfilled than simply following the curriculum.

Building Your Wealth

> ....
> "Wealth is the slave of a wise man.
> The master of a fool."
> - Seneca
> ....

Wealth will not come to you naturally. It will take hard work, dedicated focus and providing a lot of value to the world. There are of course many types of wealth - inner, financial, relationship, success, and health to name a few. Really, you can take any aspect of your life and provide a wealth value to it. Let's take a quick look at just a couple of them.

Inner Wealth - To build your inner wealth, you must work on your mindset, internal peace, and spirituality.

Financial Wealth- To build your financial wealth - focus on the 3 buckets, provide more value to people to gain more money, compound your interests in assets.

Relationship Wealth - Invest in your family, friends, spouses, and business relationships - help them grow and improve their lives - spend time with them.

Success Wealth- Your success is your own vision. How close are you to achieving your wildest visions for your life? Are you getting there in the best way possible?

Health Wealth - Are you in a peak physical and mental state? Do you have the ability to get yourself to that state?

The most important part of creating wealth is that you can then leverage it to get other things you want in your life. Financial wealth allows you to buy things, health wealth allows you to be adventurous and explore the world and inner wealth helps you get closer to figuring out exactly why you were put on this earth.

Leverage your various wealth areas wisely for they can be depleted at a much faster rate than they are built up.

Debt

Debt is a kind of a strange thing. It allows you to purchase or do things that you otherwise couldn't do, at least immediately. And sometimes that's fun or sounds like a good idea, but you have to be extremely careful what you use your credit for.

I was always so risk averse growing up, I rarely spent any money and saved quite a bit. It's a tactic that I want to try and engrain in you because even though you may want the latest and greatest thing, it will be quite short lived compared to building your wealth.

I remained that way for quite a long time, I paid for half of my brand new truck up front with cash that I had saved. I went to community college and paid for it up front at the beginning of each semester (I do moderately regret not going away to college, but I had plenty of fun experiences visiting friends).

The point I'm really getting at is that you should always try to pay for things immediately if you can. If you can't manage to do that and it's not an absolute necessity -- think the latest gaming system or television- then you should wait until you have the cash to pay for it in whole. Following this method will also help you try to figure out how to negotiate great prices because you won't want to pay as much up front.

Here's my advice:

When it's a good time to take on debt

There are times when it's a good idea to take on debt, though they will be few and far between. Below is a partial list of when I'd be ok with you taking on debt.

When debt might be ok
- Buying a home - buy it so it has equity in it already, you can't count on the market to build that equity for you.
- Affordable transportation - We all need to get around, but you don't need to buy a $90,000 car when you're working for minimum wage. Buy something that's affordable and reliable.
- Education - If it's going to pay off in the future, whether it's formal or informal education, it's always a good idea to invest in yourself.
- Things where you'll save money in the long run & can calculate it, not just speculate - We bought a pellet stove for the house. It cost us over $5,000 to buy it, get it installed and get pellets the first season, but it will pay for itself in oil savings in under 3 years, so that was a smart purchase.

When you need to avoid debt
- Latest and greatest thing - There will always be marketers trying to sell you crap. Don't buy all of it. It will be short lived and you'll have to buy the next new thing in a few months.
- Credit cards - They are life suckers. It's easy to swipe a card and get anything you want, but the debt will add up and up until it's difficult to pay it off. Try to use cash as much as possible or make sure you have the cash to cover your purchase.

Always try to pay off your credit card balance each month.
- ✦ Raiding your retirement accounts - Don't ever dip into those accounts. They are meant for your future, not to cover todays expenses. When that cash isn't in those accounts, it's not working for you to build your net worth.

Having debt will limit your ability to do things, the less debt you have the more you can do. When it comes to money, there's a lot to learn, especially when you begin looking at building your future rather than just surviving today. At the end of the day, you're going to be responsible for your financial future, nobody else is, so learn how to properly manage your money and build it up so you never have to worry about making ends meet.

I could write an entire book about proper money management, but plenty of other people have already done that. Seek out the reliable resources and learn from them as much as you can. Invest in yourself first, then you can use some of your extra money to have fun, buy frivolous things and exploit everything great about the economy.

Money

There are three basic rules to follow with money. These rules will make your life a heck of a lot easier when you understand them and follow them. You're going to make mistakes with your money, that's a given and really part of the learning process of receiving more than you output, but you'll figure it out.

When I first got hired as a dispatcher I thought I was the king. I was making WAY more money than any of my friends and I was right out of high school, it was a great job. I went out and bought a car, albeit a used one, but it wasn't really a necessary purchase. A few years later and I still thought I was hot stuff, I went out and bought a brand new truck, putting half down. I love my truck, but it was an expensive purchase, and looking back, I could have used that money to make way more money if I understood the core principles that surround money. So here we go:

1. Pay yourself first
2. Whenever possible, don't take on debt
3. Money is attracted to value

That's it. Every paycheck you get, take at least 15% for yourself, put it into a savings account, retirement account or use it to fund an investment. That money will become your foundation for the future, and remember, you're the only one responsible for your future self, don't count on someone else.

Don't take on debt. This one is important, yes there is good debt to take on, but that's few and far between. You don't need the latest gaming system, or the most expensive vehicle you can find. Those things will put you in a situation where you owe someone else, and guess what? They like to charge you for taking their money, which means whatever you bought just got more expensive instantly. Avoid debt at all costs and you'll never have to worry about owing on something you barely care about.

Money is attracted to value. You want more money right? We all do, but most people aren't willing to put in the extra effort to figure out where they can add more value. I'm not talking about taking more hours and just dumping your entire life into a place, instead, how can you become more valuable? What could you do, learn or help someone with that would make you more of an asset to the company? Money tends to follow those that continuously provide more value to the world than they try to take. Follow that path and you'll see money come your way.

Investing

Investing can be complicated, but it doesn't always need to be. In fact, if you stand by a few simple rules when you invest, you could end up making a small fortune. It will take discipline and you'll have to remove your emotions, relying instead on your knowledge and the limits you set for yourself. I'm not going to get into <u>all</u> kinds of investment terms here because I feel like I'd be wasting time and space. I'm confident you can find all the resources you need to understand how to invest. I'd rather talk to you about the core methods I've used in my life and why they work.

Learn about it – You're not going to have a clue what anyone is talking about when you get started, I know I didn't. But if I didn't know what a term was, or didn't fully understand it, I went online and found the answer I was looking for, it really is that easy.

Understand it – Make sure you fully understand what you're talking about and how each part fits into the bigger scheme of things. On the core, things are relatively simple, but if you start dabbling in more complex things, one little number could have a massive effect on your return.

Try it – Once you learn about it and understand at least the basics, you need to try it.

Dividends – I love to buy dividend paying stocks because they give me free money. I then take those funds and put them into what's called a DRIP (dividend reinvestment program) and use that money to buy more stock, all for free.

Compound interest – The power of compound interest is what makes investing so important to start when you're young. Interest earned continues to compound, growing your worth ever faster.

Compounding Effect

Everything in your life compounds. That's why it's so important to start working on things sooner than later. In investing, your interest compounds meaning you get more money for free. In life, your knowledge compounds meaning you can achieve more. In your health, your physical fitness compounds so you can live healthier. In relationships, your love and affection compounds so you can be happier and more loved. In your friendships, your time and experiences compound so you become closer friends.

Everything compounds in some way. So get started and continue to work towards the things you want most in your life. They will compound and become better and better every day.

Being Held Up

School systems are traditionally designed to hold you up. To keep you afloat until you reach this certain pinnacle they call graduation. The reality is that other than your family, there is no safety net in life. When you fail, you can fail hard. I don't say that to be negative, but to be realistic. You have a lot of responsibility on your shoulders to be able to support yourself and grow your life into what you want it to be.

While you're in school, don't take the lazy man's way and do just enough to get by. I did that for a very long time, and it made breaking free from traditional employment that much harder for me. My entire adult life was focused on responding to people's problems and fixing them, not being proactive and creating what I wanted to have. Focus your energy on being proactive, get ahead of what the world is going to throw at you, it's the only sure way to gain success.

Accountability

School serves a lot of great purposes. While they focus on so many of the academics and ensuring you can spell and know your angles, most schools never really force you to take full accountability for your life. Sure, you can get an F on an assignment, but how does that translate into the real world? It doesn't. There's a serious disconnect between education and preparing you to thrive in the real world. I'm not saying your education is a joke or you don't need it, you certainly do. But you need to put effort into figuring out how to make it in the real world too.

Everything you do, or for that matter, fail to do in life has a direct impact on your ability to survive or thrive. Once you leave the confines of high school, you're going to be responsible for yourself in ways you never had to worry about before. There will be stumbling blocks and things will get in the way, but that's part of life, figure them out and move on. You must keep moving forward, push yourself, find solutions and keep going because there is nobody there to pick up the slack when you don't follow through.

Buy Quality Things

A lot of people love to preach sales and buying the everything at a discount. I'd like to challenge that idea. Buy for quality. Don't be afraid to invest more money into better quality things. You'll have to buy less because things last longer, taste better, are stronger, you get the idea. Don't try to get everything for a discount, that's usually like buying out of the bottom of a barrel. It's nice that people can do it, but it's a fools game.

Adding Value To The World

Traditional education never teaches you how to really add value to the world. There are so many more opportunities available to you beyond just getting a normal job. And heck, you can add value to the world even outside of your job life.

Adding value is really quit simple on the surface. Find a problem that people have, and find a way to solve it. That's it. That's how you create value. Now of course it gets far more complicated than that when you really dive into the work, but that's where reading the rest of this book helps, and continuing to pursue your own, self guided education, especially if it's outside of the confines of traditional school systems.

Goal Setting

Setting your own goals is a hugely valuable skill for you to learn. But even beyond just setting goals for yourself, you need to learn how to follow through on them so you can succeed in everything you do.

Here's how I've done it for years. It may not be what works for you, but it's a valuable starting point.

1. Keep a notebook. – I use mine for daily goal setting, daily gratitude and other notes.
2. Write down just 5-10 things you want to get done. I write down many of the things I'm going to do every day anyways, like walking the dogs, writing this book, etc. It always feels good to cross things off your list that you got done. But write down 1 or 2 bigger things you must get done.
3. Work your way through the list – It helps if you can establish habits or rituals to get these things done, but if not, you at least have a solid list to work from.
4. Anything you don't get done that day (it's ok to not get every single thing done), gets moved to the next days list.
5. Try not to keep moving the same task day after day after day. At some point you either have to buckle down and get it done or realize that it's just not that important to you and to let it go from your to-do list. I've let things persist for weeks before, it slows you down and drains you more mentally than just pushing through and getting it done.
6. At the end of each day, write down 3-5 things you're grateful for. They can be simple like the sun or rain, or more complex like an amazing moment you experienced that day. This helps keep you grounded and makes you appreciate life a lot more as it's happening.

There Is No Such Thing As A Perfect Life

One of the biggest revelations I've had is that even the world's most successful people struggle. They have doubts, fears and anxiety about the things they're doing. Listening to Tim Ferriss, I understood that all these people we idolize and think are living these perfect lives have their own struggles. They aren't perfect. That took so much stress off of me thinking I wasn't capable of achieving great things. Of course I'm capable. If these people can fight through their own self doubt and internal fears, then I know I can do the same thing.

You should realize that too. You're going to have doubts and troubles along your life path, but you can get through them, everyone can. People that make excuses are just creating a reason that they can't succeed rather than getting started and pushing themselves to make it through those problems.

So while there is no such thing as a perfect life, because life wouldn't really be worth living without learning, growing and pushing ourselves, we can actually set ourselves up for huge successes. You have an incredible ability to make everything you want in life come to fruition. It will take hard, relentless and determined work to make it happen, but you can do that. It's just a matter of how badly you want it.

"Don't ever let somebody tell you... You can't do something. Not even me. All right? You got a dream. You gotta protect it. People can't do somethin' themselves, they wanna tell you you can't do it. If you want somethin', go get it. Period." - Chris Gardner - The Pursuit of Happiness

Avoid Shift Work

If at all possible during your life, avoid shift work. Your mother and I have both done it for years, and while our jobs have been great to us and provided us a lot of opportunities, working rotating hours has not been. Working regular hours may seem boring but it actually allows you to develop real and lasting success habits. Rotating working hours never allows you to settle on daily rituals that you can use to get yourself in the zone. You'll find yourself not getting enough rest, not eating the right things and much more exhausted than if you were working 'normal business' hours.

Brain Training

If you want to expand your thinking ability, and you want to be able to come up with amazing ideas, you have to train your mind to be able to do that. What James Altucher suggests doing is creating lists of ideas. It could be lists about anything you want – how to change your life, ways to make money, book ideas, vacation ideas - whatever you're working on.

If you strive for ten items on your list, the first few will come incredibly easy, all the rest will require your mind to think harder and deeper. Getting into that thinking zone is where your mind grows and changes, because rather than sitting back and waiting for life to happen to you, you're now using your mind to think of alternatives. The more you do this, the easier it gets and the better your thinking process will be.

Train your mind to think for itself – to come up with brilliant ideas and you'll never be stuck with that lost feeling for long.

The Money Isn't Worth It

The money isn't worth it if you're completely miserable. A broken spirit is far more expensive to fix than the luxuries you can buy with money.

Warren Buffet Principles

<u>On earning:</u> Never depend on single income. Make investment to create a second source.

<u>On Spending:</u> If you buy things you do not need, soon you will have to sell things you need.

<u>On savings:</u> Do not save what is left after spending, but spend what is left after saving.

<u>On taking risk:</u> Never test the depth of river with both feet.

<u>On expectations:</u> Honesty is a very expensive gift. Do not expect it from cheap people.

Warren Buffett's Rules to Riches

1. Reinvest your profits: Don't be tempted to spend your profits, reinvest the profits instead. Even a small sum can turn into great wealth.
2. Be willing to be different: Don't base your decisions upon what everyone is saying or doing. Judge yourself by your own standards.

3. Never suck your thumb: Gather in advance any information you need to make a decision. Swiftly make up your mind and act on it.

4. Spell out the deal before you start: Your bargaining leverage is always greatest before you begin when you have something to offer.

5. Watch small expenses: Be obsessive over the tiniest costs. Exercising vigilance over every expense can make you profits.

6. Limit what you borrow: Living on credit cards and loans won't make you rich. When you're debt-free, save some money for investments.

7. Be persistent: With tenacity and ingenuity, you can win against a more established competitor.

8. Know when to quit: Know when to walk away from a loss, and don't let anxiety fool you into trying again.

9. Assess the risk: Asking "and then what?" can help you see all of the possible consequences when making a decision.

10. Know what success really means: Measure success by how many of the people you want to have love you, actually do love you.

Don't Waste

Don't waste. I'm not talking about just material things or food.

Don't waste your time.
Don't waste your energy.
Don't waste your passion.
Don't waste your youth.
Don't waste your abilities.

That list can go on forever.
Instead, take full advantage of everything.

Take full advantage of your time.
Take full advantage of your energy.
Take full advantage of your passion.
Take full advantage of your youth.
Take full advantage of your abilities.

Payoff

The payoff may not be immediate. In fact, most of the time it won't be. You'll invest mountains of hard work, struggles, effort and failures to reach your goals. Rarely do those goals show themselves immediately. Keep pushing. Work through the difficult times, never give up. Your success may be just around the corner.

I once heard a story of a gold miner, who dug and dug for years. He got little bits and pieces here and there, but never hit the big jackpot that he had hoped for. He eventually sold off the land and headed back home. Within a few days, the new owners of the land struck a vein and found millions of dollars in gold. Had the original miner just pushed a little bit further instead of giving up, he would have succeeded.

Keep pushing yourself when you know you're in pursuit of something great.

Equity

If you make investments to try and make money, or even if you purchase a home, don't count on the market building equity into it for you. Only buy things that have clear equity already in them. Essentially you're buying at a discounted price from the real value. And on that note. New cars are never a good investment, they lose mountains of value nearly immediately.

Afterword

For Ben and Matt, I hope this book gives you an amazing head start on life when you're able to read it and fully comprehend everything I wrote to you. It's taken me decades to learn much of this, and my journey is only really beginning to unfold as I design and live the lifestyle I want for myself and our family.

For all the others that have read Letters To Ben, thank you for investing your time in the book and in yourself. I hope that in some small way this book has helped inspire you to live a better and more fulfilling life. Like I said in the book, it will take a lot of deliberate and dedicated effort to make it happen, but it's soooo incredibly worth it when you start down that path.

Invest in yourself each and every day and you'll quickly begin to see results that you can be proud of. Let the naysayers live in their own world, because you're a visionary, a thinker and a creator. So get out there, inspire the world with your passions, your happiness and with that person you truly are. They've been waiting for you.

I'll finish with a short story, but one that's incredibly relevant.

There was a young boy who grew up in the country, not far from a small city. Throughout his life he found so many things he was interested in, yet none of them seemed to truly fulfill him. He always worked hard and gave everything his all, but after a while he would lose interest in those things that once got him curious.

Each day he would take a walk in the woods and stare in wonder of all the amazing things around him. The wildlife, the saplings, the bed of leaves that crunched under his feet. He would sit for a long time and take in the fresh air and the views around him, sitting there wishing and hoping he would find that one thing that inspired him and motivated him.

That boy would grow up one day, and he kept working hard. Harder than ever before. He would sacrifice to make ends meet and always as he thought he was on the cusp of finding that passion that would light him up, it would invariably fizzle out.

He began an incredible journey of self-discovery hoping that he could somehow figure out what he was put here to do. Digging deeper and deeper, the years strolled by but he never felt any closer. He went down even more rabbit holes thinking he found his passion time and time again always emerging with an empty feeling inside.

He would return to the woods day after day, sometimes for long walks, other times for short visits to reset. And then one day it dawned on him that his true passion had been there all along. That one thing he kept returning to day after day to ground his life was his passion. He had been so blinded to it, instead following the whims of society that he missed his calling for years and years.

The legend goes that we were all put here on earth to focus on something, to leave this world a better place. And while it's true that the world can survive and keep on going even if we never find that passion project that lights us up each and every day, it's not nearly as complete of a place.

Imagine for a moment a world filled with people following their passions, lit up and excited to make the world a better place every single day. That's a place I want to live, and it's a reality I think we're getting closer and closer to each and every day.

Don't be afraid to follow your passions.
Light up the world in a way that is uniquely your own.

Quote Garden

Because we can all use a little inspiration, motivation and passion in our daily lives.

"Work finally begins when the fear of doing nothing exceeds the fear of doing it badly."
– Alain de Botton

"The greatest gift you can give others is the gift of your own happiness. Everything else is irrelevant if you're not whole and you're not happy." - Jesse Elder

"Words don't teach, experiences teach." - Jesse Elder

"Who you are speaks so loudly that I cannot hear what you say." - Rumi

"Knowing yourself and what you're here for will shine through so much that you can't mute it." - Unknown

"Life gives you defining moments, and it's during those defining moments that we can make choices about how our life is going to be." - Jesse Elder

"The difference in life is really just the difference in standards and expectation." Jesse Elder

"Rational fears keep you alive, irrational fears keep you from living." - Jesse Elder

"Either write something worth reading or do something worth writing." - Benjamin Franklin

"Make a decision to get in the top 10%." - Brian Tracy

"Willing is not enough; we must apply. Willing is not enough; we must do." - Bruce Lee

"A goal is not always meant to be reached, it often serves simply as something to aim at." - Bruce Lee

"Those who are unaware they are walking darkness will never seek the light." - Bruce Lee

"If you always put limits on everything you do, physical or anything else, it will spread into your work and into your life. There are no limits. There are only plateaus, and you must not stay there, you must go beyond them."
- Bruce Lee

"To hell with circumstances, I create opportunities."
- Bruce Lee

"TO LIVE IS THE RAREST THING IN THE WORLD. MOST PEOPLE EXIST, THAT IS ALL." - Oscar Wilde

"Go out and be great - and never apologize for it."
- Brendan Burchard

"Luck is what happens when preparation meets opportunity." - Seneca

"Difficulties strengthen the mind, as labor does the body." - Seneca

"Begin at once to live, and count each separate day as a separate life." - Seneca

"No man was ever wise by chance" - Seneca

"Being busy is most often used as a guise for avoiding the few critically important but uncomfortable actions."

- Tim Ferriss

Developing wisdom is not done solely for the betterment of ourselves, but rather to use that wisdom in a way that also betters the greater good of man.

www.ingramcontent.com/pod-product-compliance
Lightning Source LLC
Chambersburg PA
CBHW070738160426
43192CB00009B/1488